W9-CQS-940

Pearls of Heart Wisdom

For Living a Life You Love

∾

Tanai Starrs

Joy Heart Corporation

P.O. Box 8039 • Asheville, NC 28814

Published by
Joy Heart Corporation
P.O. Box 8039
Asheville, NC 28814
800-996-3024

Copyright© 2001 by Tanai Starrs. All rights reserved. No part of this publication may be reproduced or distributed in any form or by any means, or stored in a data base or retrieval system, without the prior written permission of the publisher.

The purpose of this book is to educate. It is sold with the understanding that the publisher and author shall have neither liability nor responsibility for any injury or alleged injury to be caused directly or indirectly by the information contained in this book. Each person's health, spiritual, emotional, mental, and creative needs are unique. To obtain recommendations appropriate to your particular situation, please consult a qualified competent professional.

Library of Congress Cataloging-in-Publication Data:

Starrs, Tanai.
   Pearls of Heart Wisdom / Tanai Starrs.
      p. cm.

   ISBN 0-9711415-4-1 Pbk.
   1. Self Help   2. Inspirational   3. Heart   4. Spirituality
I.   Title
2001 133090

Book and Cover Design by Leslie Petrovich
Editors Rebecca Reitmeyer, Regina Reitmeyer, and Leslie Petrovich

Printed in the United States of America

This book is dedicated to all who desire
life to be sweet, abundant, and fulfilling.
May their hearts flourish.

Table of Contents

Loving Myself—It's the Best

Sweet-Talking to Myself

Easy Pearls of Wisdom

Feeding My Heart

Listening With My Heart

God's Innernet

Feelings, Feelings, Feelings

What's Inside Me Pops Outside

Creating What I Love

Parents and the Heart

Too Much, Too Fast

Our Minds and Stress

Rebellion, Arrogance, and Intolerance

Bridge Between My Mind and Heart

Eliminating Fear, Victimization, and Frantic Feelings

Keeping What I Love

Acknowledgments

I thank the many people who helped me create this book. Editing: Rebecca Reitmeyer and Regina Reitmeyer. Editing, layout, and cover: Leslie Petrovich.

I thank the many supporters of The Mastery of the Heart School. It is through their love and faith in me that I have had the privilege to develop and test some of the truths presented in this book. I especially acknowledge Celeste Lauren; Joseph and Sara Malinak, Carol Lani and Jerry Johnson, Anna and Robert Murri, Michele and Michael Murphy, Charles and Joan Hunter, Teresa Vollmecke, and Danielle Earley for their consistent and loving support of me and my school; and Stephanie and John Hogge who believed in and provided enthusiastic support for this book.

I acknowledge Bill O'Donnell, Jr. for his love. I honor my friend Debra Mills who helped me create the title of this book while we sat on the deck of a boat waiting for dolphins to invite us into the sea to play.

I thank my son, Craig, who is a great blessing and teacher to me. Our love has always been a powerful fuel for my creativity.

Preface

My desire to write this book began over sixteen years ago. I had an enormous passion to share the sacred truths I was learning about living with an open and trusting heart. I discussed this with a wise friend who assured me that even though my enthusiasm was enormous and my confidence equal to it, I would be unsuccessful at sharing my knowledge through books until I matured in wisdom.

She told me I was not ready, for she felt my soul had carefully arranged my life so that I would not be able to share my knowledge and wisdom with humanity until it had matured more deeply. With impatience and arrogance, I explained to her that she was wrong in this case and that my passion would create and publish my book within months. She smiled at me with the same smile that I give my students when their enthusiasm far exceeds their maturity.

I now write this book sixteen years later, with the seasoning of wisdom that comes from many life experiences and the ups and downs they bring. My wisdom comes from inner knowledge that was garnered from life's lessons. My love of God and my passion to serve held me on course until the ups and downs revealed better ways of using knowledge to create the love, abundance, and sweetness that life has available for all of us through our hearts. I know that my acquired wisdom benefits my students whether I meet them through The Mastery of the Heart School or through my seminars. Their lives change positively and rapidly as they absorb this wisdom into their lives.

Often, my students have introduced me to their friends by saying, "You'll never be the same again." Later, the introduced person laughs as my teachings quickly help them to experience and create what they want and love in life. My heart would love for this book to have the same effect on you.

Many of the truths I share with you I learned through diverse, intense, and often difficult life lessons. My goal is to navigate you through a potentially challenging passageway to love, which you might have missed or which might have taken you, as it did me, years to get through. Rather than you spending years struggling, these Pearls of Heart Wisdom are signposts that guide you to the deep richness within you.

In this book, I wanted to touch the heart of humanity to assist them in their daily lives. Our hearts have been burdened with too much for too long. My heart desired my wisdom to be given to you in a way that feels safe, entertaining, and close. For that reason, I chose this simple format of pearls of wisdom taught through personal anecdotes. I have known for years that an intimate and loving bond between humanity and me is one of my soul's greatest desires.

You will notice that I have often used these characters in the text: . . . to encourage you to slow down your reading and take a short break to ponder the information and questions. It is through your willingness to explore inside yourself that you unlock the potential of this information to bless your daily life.

My heart sends to you bright blessings and a sincere desire that your life be greatly enhanced through reading *Pearls of Heart Wisdom: For Living a Life You Love.*

—Tanai Starrs

Loving Myself—It's the Best

Pearl One

Loving Myself as Much as My Animals

Recently I taught a workshop at a university in Colorado. Although my heart has desired to teach university students the principles of self-love for many years, this was my first opportunity to teach on their territory. During the workshop, I explored how to use simplified teachings from The Mastery of the Heart School I cofounded. Although I could feel that they were listening, their defenses about self-love were keeping them from really understanding what my heart wanted to share with them. I knew I had to find a way to reach them, or they would leave the workshop with information that would have little impact in their lives.

I suddenly knew the way to reach the students. I asked them to feel how much they loved their animals. The room immediately filled with smiles and bright inward light that made love real and tangible for everyone. Pleased, I paused to allow everyone to feel the richness of their love. Several students looked at one another to share how much they loved their animals. As everyone was basking in the pouring of love into the room, I softly and slowly shared, "*Self-love* feels like this, and it is all about *you loving you*. Self-love feels like you loving yourself as much as you love your animals." It was at that moment that the class opened up to the possibility of self-love.

The students had shocked looks on their faces. Not once in their eighteen to twenty-two years had it ever occurred to them to love themselves as much as they love their animals—or, for that matter, anything else. The gap in their understanding of love was so huge that none of them had ever dared to risk creating or experiencing this level of self-love.

As the shock of the possibility of self-love moved through their bodies, I could feel their sense of betrayal over not being taught to love themselves but rather being tricked into believing they were supposed to avoid self-love. After their betrayal feelings passed, I sensed their confusion. They were uncertain about how to love themselves.

It was at this point that they each moved to the edge of their seats and leaned as close as they could to me in order to deeply drink in the teachings of self-love. When I completed the class, I felt that almost half of the students had shifted their destinies towards seeking and desiring self-love as a way of life.

Study your world. Do you give yourself permission to love yourself? . . 🌹 . . Do you feel self-love is selfish and inappropriate? . . 🌹 . . It is your ability to love yourself that feeds and nourishes you and helps you create a world that blesses you. Self-love does not diminish your ability to love others. Self-love is a way of relating to yourself that brings all good things to you. True self-love creates healthy ways of loving others by using your love for yourself as the foundation for loving others.

Are you willing to allow greater self-love into your life? . . 🌹 . . If you do allow it, your life will become fulfilling and more blessed. That's how it works. The more you love yourself, the more your life works and feels good. That's what this book is about. *Pearls of Heart Wisdom* are simple anecdotal lessons about opening your heart to create greater self-love to enable your life to blossom with warmth, abundance, and well-being.

Pearl Two

My Mind Supporting My Heart

I used to live in a condo complex in St. Simons Island, Georgia. I would sit outside on my patio shaded by huge oak trees and watch a beautiful four-year-old girl run and play. Although I never chatted with her, I knew she was my teacher. Often she talked out loud to herself, so I could hear what she was perceiving, thinking, and feeling. This little girl was truly centered in her heart. Miraculously, she had not shut her heart down or had any of the signs of diminishing self that come from a defended and insecure heart.

When she ran, I would hear her say, "I am the best runner in the whole world. I love how I run." There was no competitiveness or desire to prove or defend anything. She knew she was the best runner, because her heart could feel the joy of her running. When the other kids would run faster than she, it did not make any difference to her. Her running allowed her to fully experience what an amazing being she was. She knew how special she was, not from feedback from others or competing with other children, but through the joy she experienced as she lived.

I loved watching her. As her long blonde hair flowed to the ground while she hung upside down on the swing set, I would hear the confidence of a secure heart speaking. Her mind was always supporting her well-being and assisting her in feeling confident and loved in every situation. Her wide-open heart could trust, moment by moment, that words of love, support, and encouragement were always there for her. The words of reassurance were coming from her, and she had an unlimited supply of these words of appreciation.

She amazed me. My mind had been trained at a young age to do the opposite through criticizing myself. It was always denying and undercutting my support, appreciation, and encouragement. As a result, my heart felt fearful and insecure.

When my mind says unkind and critical things about me, I now say, "Stop, Sweetie, you're hurting me. These critical words hurt my heart. Say nice things to me that show how much you value me. I deserve it, and it opens my heart and lets me feel safe."

Because my mind had said so many mean things to me, my heart simply didn't trust my mind. Why should it? It had hurled mean criticism at me for much of my life. As my mind learns to be kinder and more tender to me, my heart is learning to trust and relax. This allows my life to feel more secure and tender. My heart feels safe to stay open, which in turn makes me feel full and abundant. I don't feel I need to defend and protect myself so much which makes everything easier and more relaxed.

Watch your thoughts. Does your mind provide thoughts of encouragement, appreciation, and valuing for yourself? . . . . . If so, you are blessed as this little girl was. If not, then perhaps you can begin the process of teaching your mind to support your heart.

The next time you criticize yourself, gently tell your mind to stop hurting yourself. Let your mind understand that criticism hurts your precious heart. Then let your heart teach your mind how to say loving supportive words in sweet tones. As you do this, your mind will learn to love to support you in this tender way and your heart will purr with joy.

Pearl Three

Speaking From My Heart

I taught a workshop in Florida called *Creating Your Heart's Desire*. The focus of this workshop is to help students feel and create what their hearts desire. Once they can identify their true heart feelings, I teach them how to create their chosen project or desired manifestation.

Normally, I sit on the same level as my students. In this particular workshop, I told them that I would be staying on the stage. I soon discovered why.

In this workshop, I was speaking from my heart very openly about my creative abilities. My heart was very full and beautiful. I was loving myself and was very expressive and passionate about what I love about myself. This is a very powerful place inside all of us that is free of ego and arrogance. My heart was simply loving itself and allowing my students to feel what a heart loving itself feels like. I was not puffing myself up from insecurity, but instead giving my heart full permission to express its love for me.

This felt so good to me that I decided to have my students do the same thing. So I asked them to speak about what they loved about themselves. Instantly, every one of them shrunk in their chairs and tried to disappear.

They had been taught that it was inappropriate to value, love, and communicate what they loved about themselves. They had been trained to hide who they are and to withhold sharing the fullness of their love for themselves. As each one spoke, they were weak-voiced and insecure and tried to fake that they were less than the beautiful and talented beings I knew they really were. As they shrunk in their chairs, they compressed their physical hearts, making an open heart physically difficult.

So I asked each one to come up one at a time. Standing on the stage, I had them open their bodies up and allow the beauty of their hearts to openly express what they loved about themselves. Eventually, each one learned to open his or her heart and feel the freedom of loving and acknowledging one's heart.

The instant they transitioned from hiding their love to opening their hearts to fully express their love for themselves, the group lit up. Everyone loved being a part of so much expressed love.

It was wonderful to see the students express love for themselves, their hearts, and their abilities. The minute they would close their hearts and deny their love for themselves, the group would shrink back and lose their huge smiles and heart pleasure. When one student denied his or her heart, the group's joy diminished. As each expressed self-love, we all felt that expressed love.

Before the workshop, the students perceived that they would not be loved if they expressed their love for themselves or let others see their full abilities. They believed that it was inappropriate to allow others to see their self-love, because it might make others feel bad about themselves. As they expressed this, I realized that in our social structure, many individuals deny their hearts and their abilities because of a belief system that is based on diminishing self so that others are comfortable about diminishing themselves. This keeps us all in a confined box that hurts everyone.

Our hearts love to value us. Our hearts also love to share in the richness and joy of others valuing their hearts. When we each value our love for ourselves, everyone is uplifted into the power and fullness of the heart.

Suggestion: Invite a friend whom you trust to support you speaking about your love for yourself. Until you break through this fear-barrier, you are limiting your ability to love yourself and create what you love. Once you break through this barrier and openly express your love for yourself, new doorways unlock to greater self-love for you.

Epilogue: The love built to such a powerful level in this workshop that everyone manifested their dream project within a few months—such as conceiving a baby with a low probability, several buying new homes, and losing weight. That is how powerful self-love is!

Pearl Four

When I Need Love the Most

Several years ago I watched an important football game on TV. In the last minute of play, the receiver missed the ball that would have won the game for his team. This player had put all he had in his attempt to catch the ball, and he simply had not been successful. He stormed off the playing field and marched up and down the sidelines driving hate, rage, and punishment towards himself.

I knew that his behavior was damaging his heart. This, in turn, was reducing his ability to catch the next crucial play, creating so much internal pain that a part of him would prefer quitting than enduring so much punishment, and leaving himself depleted and unacknowledged for his effort and desire to catch that ball for himself, his teammates, and his fans. With the massive aggression of a powerful football player, he was attempting to punish and destroy himself in front of his TV audience. It hurt to watch him.

He thought he was supposed to hate and punish himself with self-directed brutal rage at the very moment he deserved and needed the most love from himself, his teammates, and his fans. He didn't know that self-love would have comforted him and provided the confidence to be more likely next time to succeed in the crucial play.

Self-love would have created the safety of knowing that he would be loved whether he made the star play or not. When individuals know they are going to receive love whether they win or not, they relax and allow all of their abilities to support their endeavors. Deep within him he would fear for the rest of his life that he would miss the play and afterwards be cruel and self-destructive. This player simply didn't know that self-love would have greatly increased his odds of success at the next crucial moment and thereby uplift the quality of his life.

If self-love had been taught to this player, he would have immediately started comforting himself the instant he realized he had missed the crucial play that his heart so desired to make. He would have known at that moment of enormous disappointment that he would need and deserve his greatest expression of love for himself.

Had he been able to generate enough self-love at that moment of great despair deep within himself, he would have learned that he could trust himself to be there for himself with love no matter what occurs. This knowing that you can always be there for yourself with self-love is a place of great safety that powerfully reduces crippling fear. With enough self-love his teammates, press, and coaches would have been there to acknowledge his huge effort and compassionately help him through his disappointment. Through loving himself, he would have received the reward of learning how much everyone cares about him, even when he isn't successful.

Unfortunately, through his self-punishment and unwillingness to love himself, he probably experienced separation from his teammates, coaches, and fans. He might have been sure it was because he missed the play. The truth was that he generated so much self-hatred that it would have been hard for others to get through this in order for him to feel they cared.

His self-generated hatred probably caused him to be mean, critical, and resentful of the press and those around him. As he created being an enemy of himself, the hatred would quickly spread so that he would perceive those around him as his enemies. The pain of this cycle is unbearable, and people of all walks of life are creating it every day. They will not allow others to love them because they are so busy punishing and hating themselves.

Had this player really loved himself, chances are much greater that he would not have missed the play in the first place. As violent as this player was to himself, he had probably attacked himself many times before.

Had he supported self-love, the minute that the crucial play was forming, he could have relaxed into an abundance of self-love to provide the connecting and unifying energies to bring that ball securely into his hands for the touchdown. As he was extending for the ball, his heart could stay open and expansive knowing that he was creating love for himself regardless of the outcome. At that moment, he would have been *playing the game for love,* because he would receive love regardless of what happened. He would be secure in this, not because of how others would treat him, but through knowing that his love for himself was so expansive that if he missed the ball, he would give himself extra, extra love.

That loving, relaxed, warm self-love would have created the situation of highest probability of experiencing love which would have been catching the ball and being the hero. It could only be created from loving himself. Without this type of self-love, his heart was in terror that he would miss.

Missing for this player meant activating all his passion to destroy and hurt himself. His closed heart would assure that fear was created rather than his blessed heart's desire of winning the game. Thus, his football genius was diminished or not available to him due to his fear of cruelty to himself. Therefore, the game was lost.

Playing life for love makes it warmer, more fulfilling, and more successful. By playing life for love, you know moment by moment you are there to love and comfort yourself regardless of the outcome. If a painful life experience is created, it would be at this time that one is most loving and supportive with extra self-love.

Feel. How can you bring that kind of ever-present love into your daily life? . . ❦ . . When do you need extra, extra love? . . ❦ . . Do you give it to yourself, or do you hurl rage and punishment on yourself when you truly need extra self-love the most? . . ❦ . . Are you willing to give yourself the self-love you deserve? . . ❦ . . If you do, it will make all the difference in every aspect of your life.

Pearl Five

Loving Myself While Evolving into My Greater Self

I write this pearl for anyone who passionately pursues self-growth or a greater spiritual connection to God. My students have a passion to learn about their hearts and gain what we call self-mastery. As they gain self-mastery, they begin to study how to transform every aspect of their lives into what they love to live. They learn to see clearly what supports love and an open trusting heart in their lives, and what within them denies love, hurts them, and closes their hearts. They learn that their ability to feel love is directly linked to their ability to experience God's love.

One of their important lessons is learning how to have the passion to transform into their greater selves while still fully and patiently loving themselves each step of the way. That means loving themselves even when they think they are falling short of what their hearts seek to create and master in their lives.

Their minds may greatly desire to push and force themselves into greater expressions of self-love. However, there is a limit to how far pushing can take an individual, especially if one's desire is to experience a more trusting heart.

Ultimately, the next step in personal evolution is for the *patient heart* to say, "Relax, I love you as you are today. My abundant love is here for you regardless of what you do or what you don't do." Without the patient heart, the mind may push too hard and demand too much, which causes the heart to close.

This actually works against the very desire for more love that we seek. In our attempt to become a greater being of love, our minds can cause the heart to close in panic through its dissatisfaction and demand for us to improve ourselves. Without the heart, true perfection is impossible. A healthy heart loves itself and is pleased with its progress each step of the way.

I have learned about the healthy heart from my son. If I suggested that he do something to take himself into what I perceived as a greater expression of himself, such as seek an A instead of a B in class, he always showed me a clearer picture of a healthy heart. He consistently replied, "Mom, I really feel good about what I've accomplished. I feel I am doing enough. I am proud of myself."

When he said this, I knew that the constant striving and dissatisfaction that I created as a child to create love through seeking approval was not correct. Because I felt so unloved in my younger years, this still had power to push me beyond the loving acceptance of a healthy heart. My son's approval of himself reminded me of how a loving heart relates to itself. When he said this, I backed off from both him and myself and felt the pride of a parent raising a child who holds true to his heart.

No matter the tradition or the focus of self-growth, individuals must learn to love regardless of what they uncover or learn about themselves. When I first began my spiritual focus about twenty years ago, I remember how extremely harsh I was. My point of reference was that I must have done something wrong—what, I had no idea. Therefore, I would help God punish me when I was bad. This created tremendous pain.

The choice to evolve and learn greater expressions of yourself as a loving, spiritually aware person is a wondrous pursuit. Ultimately in this journey, you will learn to love yourself richly, even when shown patterns which do not support the love you seek. For example, if you learn that you are very critical of yourself, criticizing how critical you are only deepens the pain and does little to heal what has caused it. Loving yourself is the necessary ingredient to change these patterns to loving ones.

The fragile grooves of a vinyl record are similar to patterns of unloving behavior. Instead of carefully applying some plastic into the grove to heal yourself, you use the nail of criticism to score the record deeper. Soon, the record can only play scratchy, painful music. Attacking yourself when you discover painful patterns hurts you and retards your growth. By fixing these grooves and changing the patterns, you begin to feel and express love for yourself.

If you are self-critical, it takes much self-mastery and self-love to continue loving yourself when you perceive you have not delivered your best. In truth, in those instances when I perceived I had failed, I was learning through experiences that deny love. I could not teach as I do now had I not experienced those perceived failures. Each of us learns in our ups and downs, and often this learning has a special purpose, although we may not realize why at the time.

There is a place I go inside myself when I feel desperation, that a situation is beyond hope, or that I failed. It is a place of enormous love for God. This place is always there, no matter what the circumstances. I know this place of love for God is even greater than the pain, destruction, or inability to create what I love. It is a part of my power and is always there.

I learned about this place in a situation in which I feared I was dying. I know this place inside me is infinitely more true, real, and loving than any physical experience that hurts or harms me. Each of us has a place of faith within ourselves that is more powerful than the ups and downs of our lives. Peace comes from knowing that I can go at any time to this powerful place of solace.

Do you allow yourself to feel love for yourself, especially when you feel you have failed or created less than you had hoped? . . ✤ . . Do you judge yourself harshly in these situations, or do you shower yourself with abundant self-love, soothing, and nurturing? . . ✤ . . Are you willing to be more aware of being patient, accepting, and appreciative of each step of your personal process of life?

When we perceive we are not doing it right, have failed, or can't get it right, it is a perfect time to return to this place of truth within. As we choose to learn self-growth and self-improvement, we can learn that self-love transforms our learning experience into valuable rather than punishing lessons.

Pearl Six

Opening Up to Receiving Pleasure

While I was traveling with one of my students, we talked about her difficulty in creating intimacy. As we did, I sensed that her body was simply not open to experience pleasure with anyone. She had a history of accidents, surgeries, and emotional trauma.

I asked her to try an experiment: I told her to watch me as I lovingly rubbed my hand across my arm. I explained to her that as I did, I experienced a pleasurable feeling. I suggested that she rub her hand across her arm or leg and see if she felt pleasure from this. When she did, she shook her head with frustration indicating that this did not create a pleasurable feeling for her. If she felt anything at all, it certainly was not pleasure.

She did not realize that it was appropriate and normal for loving touch to create a pleasurable sensation. I explained to her that the cells in her body were in a chronic state of distrust and panic from so much trauma. Until she could feel pleasure through the safety of her own touch, it would be unrealistic to anticipate that her husband could go through her defenses to get any different response. She agreed.

I suggested that she work with her body to slowly retrain her cells to anticipate and allow pleasure. I recommended she use a lamb's wool powder puff, which creates wondrously pleasurable feelings, and other sensual items such as feathers and beautifully scented oils and creams. She would need to seduce her body into opening back up through pleasure. Her life experiences had trained her body to believe that touch provided pain and torture, and as a result her body was guarded and shut down. I encouraged her to focus on opening up her entire body to sensual awareness and feeling her existence on Earth as a pleasurable experience.

I explained to her that she could not push her body or herself one second faster than she could go. If she pushed, then she would validate her body's fears that the Earth is painful and that she was being forced to experience pain and torture. The slower she took this training, the faster she would be able to create the pleasure she was seeking.

Within about four months of focusing on training her body to open to pleasure, she was extremely pleased with her progress. She coached herself in a nonthreatening and nonforcing way out of the locked-up world she had lived where pleasure was not possible for her to experience. Once she could safely and easily enjoy pleasure through her own touch, she taught her husband how to relate to her in a way that was nonthreatening so that she could begin experiencing pleasure through his touch as well.

For individuals who have experienced abuse, this is a powerful way to heal the body. It was designed with the capacity for great pleasure. Trauma tricks our bodies into a world of pain, suffering, and tightness so we don't trust anymore. This can be healed with patience, tenderness, and softness with self. When you do heal, your body is free to respond with trust and openness to feel pleasure rather than pain and constriction.

Does your body naturally respond to stimulus by creating pleasure through trust and openness? . . 🌹 . . Do you limit pleasure or perceive that pleasure is only available through sexuality? . . 🌹 . . Do you maintain and groom your body in a mindless and rushed way, or do you allow this daily activity to provide openness, relaxation, and pleasure for your body? . . 🌹 . . Do you create tender touch for your body throughout the day, whether from yourself or others?

As you learn to live your life more centered in your heart, you will discover how fulfilling and pleasurable even daily activities can be.

Sweet-Talking To Myself

Pearl Seven

Sweet-Talking to Myself

I teach people how to love themselves through the tone of their voice and words they speak to themselves. With the many students I reach, they consistently are amazed that speaking to themselves with loving kindness is appropriate as well as their responsibility if they desire to experience the richness of a trusting heart.

I find that people may speak sweetly to a beautiful baby or a tender animal, but never to themselves. Many people feel they are supposed to be tough with themselves and tender with others. The truth is that we need to be tender with ourselves so we are full and healthy. It is from the fullness of self-love that we can share true tenderness and love with others.

The tones you use to speak to yourself are as important as the words. Tender tones soothe, heal, and comfort. The harshness of our fast-paced world can leave us starved for the tender tones and words that nurture.

I teach people how to say these sweet things to themselves:

Sweetie, everything is going to be all right. Don't worry. I'm here for you. I love you. I know you're disappointed. I'm here to give you extra love—as much as you desire. How can I help you? How can I show you how much I care about and love you? I value you. I love you. Let me hold you sweetly, so you can relax and trust again.

As I teach students the sweet tones and words that comfort and soothe, I love to watch the results. I had a college student who came to one of my self-love classes. Later, her mother shared that a friend in her daughter's dorm was struggling with the desire to commit suicide. The daughter told her mom that after my class she was able to soothe her friend and help her.

When her friend was suffering with her pain and self-destructiveness, my student would use the same tone of voice I did and tell her, "Sweetie, everything will be all right. It's going to be okay. Trust. Love yourself, Sweetie. You deserve all the love that you can give yourself. Everything is going to be fine." Sharing these simple phrases with loving tones, she saw amazing results. She was teaching her friend how to love herself, as I had taught her.

Another student loved to hold her eighteen-month-old son and soothe and comfort him with the words and tones she had learned from me. One day, she walked into a room to see her son holding their cat like a baby saying, "Don't worry, Kitty. Love yourself even more, Sweetie. Everything will be all right." My heart treasures this story.

Can you give this nurturing to others but not yourself? . . . It is not uncommon for individuals who are in deep need of self-love to nurture others with a futile hope they will be nurtured in return. Unfortunately, this only further increases their starvation and neediness for nurturing. Unless you learn to give yourself love, you will not be able to fully help and love others.

You are the only being in the whole universe who can give yourself *self-love*. Unless you understand that nurturing and loving yourself is your responsibility, you become needy, powerless, and codependent on others.

When I lead groups with loving tones and these soothing phrases, both men and women consistently tell me that they have never felt such nurturing in their entire lives. This amazing ability to nurture and generate kindness is inside each of us. We have simply been tricked into believing we are not supposed to give it to ourselves.

Explore. . . . Say the above phrases to yourself in sweet soothing tones, nurturing and comforting yourself. As you do, does your body easily receive the tenderness, or do you get tough and uncomfortable, believing that it is not appropriate for you to receive kindness from yourself?

Only you can create self-love. Don't miss a moment to lavish self-love upon yourself. This heals your heart and makes your life a blessing to your soul.

How do you speak to yourself when you silently listen to your thoughts or talk out loud when you perceive no one is around? . . ❧ . . Do your words convey sweetness, valuing, and honoring? . . ❧ . . Or are they harsh like striking whips that cause your heart to wince in pain? . . ❧ . . Do your words soothe, allowing you to deeply relax and trust, or do your words frighten and upset you, creating chaos? . . ❧ . . From the thoughts in your mind, do you really know that you love and value yourself? . . ❧ . . Or do your words constantly keep you insecure and feeling that you are not good enough and can never be loved for who you are?

Self-love is learned and can be taught. If you did not have the opportunity to learn this before now, use this book to open the doorway to exploring self-love as a way of life. Sweet-talking yourself is a wonderful way to begin the life journey to greater self-love.

Pearl Eight

The Language of the Heart

The language of love to me is far more than carefully selected words. In fact, the language of love is more sounds and feelings than the intellectual thoughts, concepts, or symbols normally transferred by words.

When my son was growing up, sometimes we would have long conversations using sounds rather than words. With the inflection of our aaa's and ooo's, we would share amazing stories. Both of us knew on a feeling level exactly what had occurred in our emotionally rich and dramatic stories. We loved to share these wordless stories.

For fun, sometimes we would use only "no" and "yes" to communicate. We could go on for as long as an hour in a conversation style exploring all kinds of feelings and dynamic possibilities with only these two words.

Notice lovers. They often create a language that is uniquely theirs. Their heart language usually consists of very simple sounds and words expressed in special tones with little mental significance and no intellectual value. Always their loving heart language allows them to feel connected, safe, and playful.

Some of the couples I teach have created this beautiful flow of love. No one else has the key to the translation for their heart language. It would be quite impossible for someone else to say these words to them because this language is so intimate. Their heart language is theirs and theirs alone. These couples communicate daily on this level, and it feeds their love. They never tire of it, even though it is repetitive. That is one of the ingredients of heart language.

When I teach people, I use the tone of my voice and simple soothing words to help them remember the language of their own heart. Once they feel the tenderness, sweetness, and simplicity inside themselves, they have the opportunity to open themselves to feel and create their own heart language.

The language of the heart feeds us and makes this world feel worth living. Intellectuals often have difficulty with this unless they are willing to relax their mental guard and open themselves to the language of the heart. Children naturally respond because they have not yet been trained to use their minds to deny their hearts.

When you awaken your heart language, there may be some unexpected results. Here's an example. Recently my son said to me, "Mom, do you realize that you hum when you hug me?" Smiling sheepishly, I replied, "Yes, Craig, I do." It often happens. When I hug or get close to someone I love, I hum. It's not that I plan to hum, it simply happens like a surprise smile. I know I am feeling love and my heart is safe and open because that hum is nearby. It is one of the ways I love myself through loving others.

Feel. . . 🌹. . Do you have a special heart language with yourself or someone dear? . . 🌹. . If not, are you open to creating a heart language with yourself? . . 🌹. . Is there someone special in your life, whether a friend or relative, with whom you would love to create a heart language? . . 🌹. . Are you willing to share your desire with them?

Notice that as you begin to share the desire for closeness with someone, your heart language emerges out of warm, playful feelings rather than thoughts.

Pearl Nine

Deeply Receiving a Compliment

I noticed my students would sometimes go numb when receiving a compliment or perhaps get embarrassed and pretend gratitude for the compliment. "Stop! You're faking it," I exclaimed one day. I asked a student to come to the front of the class whom I knew deserved to be acknowledged and appreciated for her contributions to planning the meals for our programs. As she stood in front of the class, I walked up beside her. I explained to the class how important I felt her contribution was. She had been able to create the quality food program, which I could not have provided. Then I gently touched her on the back of her heart and explained to her that I was going to be with her until she would allow herself to receive the love and appreciation we all felt for her.

For her to feel the compliment so it was real and appropriately supporting her, she had to remove her numbness and defenses and allow her mind to let go of control so that she could become aware of her feelings. Eventually, she was successful, and everyone clapped and sent her love and appreciation, which she was able to feel. This was an important step in her honestly sensing that she was valuable and important to each of us.

After this exercise, I noticed my other students would do the following: If they received a compliment that they did not allow themselves to feel, they would say, "I'm sorry, I didn't allow myself to feel this compliment.

Would you please repeat it for me so I don't miss it?"

Then they breathed deeply, slowing down their body and thoughts so they could focus on their feelings, which are slower than thoughts. They extended their arms out to open their chest, which helped open their heart. They looked the person giving the compliment in the eyes as they smiled, connecting fully to that person. They centered their awareness in their heart so it was open and receptive. In summary, here are the steps:

Breathe deeply
Extend your arms out a little to open your chest and heart up
  to receive
Look the person giving the compliment in the eyes
Center awareness in your heart

The one giving the compliment patiently waited, loving that the person truly wanted to experience the compliment through his or her heart and feelings. Then the student would nod that he or she was ready. The one giving the compliment smiled, knowing that the other student was doing all she or he could to be fully present to receive the compliment as it was repeated. For some, it took several tries before they gifted themselves the richness of truly feeling valued and acknowledged through the other person's compliment.

Do you allow yourself to experience a deep, rich awareness of the compliments you receive? . . ❧ . . Is your heart open and receptive, or is it closed? . . ❧ . . Do you pretend or fake a response to the compliment? . . ❧ . . Do you numb your feeling awareness by tossing the compliment out with thoughts such as, "They don't really mean this. I'm really much less than this. They're really making fun of me"?

Are you willing to practice with a friend learning to allow yourself to feel a compliment with your heart? . . ❧ . . Are you willing to heal the mean and critical thought patterns that would tell you that you are not worthy of the compliment? . . ❧ . . Do you love yourself enough to treat yourself with lavish richness by deeply feeling the love of others through the compliments they give to you?

Learning to truly feel and experience compliments is a birthright that will greatly bless and enrich your life. You are the one who chooses when you learn to receive this gift.

Pearl Ten

Criticism Hurts My Heart

In our society at the present time, few beings actually are blessed with understanding how to love themselves. We are taught to criticize and critique ourselves unrelentingly. Every time you criticize yourself, your heart attempts to protect or defend itself in some way. That is how painful criticism is to the heart! Sometimes our internal criticism is so painful that it literally creates an open wound inside the true nature of our hearts. Eventually, this will create physical heart problems.

At the beginning of one of my workshops, a college student openly expressed how angry she was at God and everything. She had been born with a defective heart and felt that it was God's fault that she had been denied a healthy one. She almost had a heart transplant, and at the last minute she improved and did not get the transplant. She was on many medications and had a pacemaker.

During the workshop, I helped her to see how her criticism and meanness toward herself was destructive to her heart. I shared that her anger was directed at herself; her sacrificial relationship patterns hurt herself, and therefore hurt her heart. I explained to her, "God's love which you feel in this workshop has the ability to heal your heart. However, if your heart was healed or a perfectly new one implanted today, within six months, the healed heart would become damaged because of your criticism and meanness toward yourself."

I could see profound shock in her face when she heard this. For the first time in her life, she understood that she had the ability to heal or to damage her heart. She realized that she had a power within herself—self-love—that had the potential to release her from being a victim of her health. She understood she had choices in the quality and wellness of her heart and life.

I saw her a few months after this workshop. She chose to do self-love work every day, and her physical life and relationships were rapidly changing. She was taking responsibility for the first time in her life for creating a healthy heart. I loved hearing her share with the other college students how profoundly her physical life was changing as a result of what she had learned about loving herself. As she learned to master her destructive criticism, she gave her heart a chance to heal. As her heart healed, so did her relationships, and her ability to create what she loved blossomed.

In our society, it is very easy to learn to be self-critical. I learned this in early childhood. I believe that none of us are victims, even though it can feel as though we are. The experiences which created my unrelenting self-criticism were deeply painful to my heart. However, the lessons I learned while healing my own mean and self-destructive criticism have been invaluable in helping others do the same.

Can you feel why you desire to criticize yourself? . . ❧ . . Perhaps, it is a pattern you can stop by recognizing that it hurts and works against you having a healthy heart and an empowered life living what you love. Do you feel that the self-criticism helps you? . . ❧ . . Are you willing to exchange the criticism for the language of self-love? . . ❧ . . Are you ready to step out of this criticism pattern and learn to love and value yourself with thoughts of love and support?

If so, practice self-love. Your heart has been patiently waiting for you to gain this understanding so its value can be restored and empowered in your life.

Pearl Eleven

Ouch! How Do I Stop My Self-Criticism?

Self-criticism damages our hearts and cripples our creative abilities. Feel it out. Do you desire to be needy, to perceive yourself as not enough, and to remain loyal to any family patterns of meanness to yourself? Unless you desire to experience life restrained by the above heavy weights, self-criticism works against you. Here's my suggestions on how to stop self-criticism:

Step 1: Recognize that you will keep self-criticism as long as you value it.

Do you perceive self-criticism benefits you? Often individuals perceive that in order to be loved, they must be perfect. They believe that to be perfect they must push and drive themselves more as they criticize and criticize. This type of perfection is shallow and painful, and leaves individuals farther from the love they were often seeking to experience in the first place. Without the heart involved in daily life, individuals actually diminish and hurt themselves. True perfection which creates deep fulfillment always involves an open and loving heart.

Because of the unrelenting criticism I experienced and the accompanying sense of not feeling loved, I worked hard to create more awards as a youth. I felt that if I could be perfect and special that I would be able to create love. Obviously, even though I expended a great amount of effort, my attempts to be perfect and special did not produce the love I was seeking.

By the end of high school, I realized perfectionism and striving for bigger and bigger successes got me no more love and left me tired and searching for a bigger goal. I knew this was not the answer, yet I was desperate for love and approval. Unfortunately, at that time I did not understand that self-love was the path to receiving the love I desired.

If you perceive that self-criticism assists you, feel why you value criticism. . .❦. . Are you striving for a perfection that jams, restricts, and prevents your heart from allowing and creating the love you desire? . .❦. . Is the perfection you seek based on a driving, dissatisfied mind?

Are you unaware of why you perceive self-criticism to be valuable? . .❦. . If you focus on finding beliefs hidden deep within you, they will show themselves to you. Often studying the patterns that cause your family members to be self-critical may help you gain awareness of deeply embedded patterns from your lineages.

Once you recognize these patterns, you can choose to keep them, or you can release them, knowing they are harmful and no longer useful to you. So often these destructive patterns come from our family lineages. Sometimes we remain loyal to them because we are fearful that it would create separation from our family if we grow beyond the self-criticism.

One of the reasons that releasing self-criticism and opening to self-love can be so frightening is that each of us becomes very powerful and creative with self-love nurturing and feeding us. If you are in a family where diminishing yourself through limiting your wealth, fulfillment, or whatever is the norm, it can feel uncomfortable breaking free. If you heal these patterns, you will be different. The truth is that you would stand as a beacon of hope for the rest. However, this takes courage and may initially incur negative responses from the ones who are deeply loyal to diminishing themselves.

Step 2: Learn to say to your mind, "Stop, you're hurting me. My heart wants you to love me."

After stopping your mind when it starts to criticize you, then show your mind how to love, value, and support your heart. An example would be showing your mind how to protect your heart with words of kindness and encouragement. The goal is to teach your mind how to protect and value your heart. As the mind understands more loving ways to treat you, your heart learns to trust and open up to your mind. Gradually, the diminishing of self that comes from self-criticism begins to acquiesce in favor of the empowerment that comes from self-love. Life has the opportunity to become warmer and easier as a result.

I discovered that any greatness I seek to express naturally flows from the fullness of my self-love. When it flows from the abundant springs of self-love, it feels good and deeply nourishes me.

What are your motivations for self-criticism? . . .✿. . .Are you ready to heal the thought and emotional patterns that create the desire for criticism of you? . . ✿. . . Are you willing to go beyond the self-criticism patterns that create pain and limitations which may have been learned from your family or social structure?

What is your plan to teach your mind to protect, support, and value your heart by ending self-criticism? . .✿. . . Is your heart willing to learn to trust and open to your mind based on your desire to eliminate self-criticism as a way of life?

Pearl Twelve

I Can't Take Any More
of Their Criticism

During my childhood and young adult years, I created a barrage of unrelenting criticism. It was harsh and unceasing. Until I was in college, I thought it was normal. In college, I began recognizing that criticism hurt me and began a rather slow process of exploring how to stop it.

I perceived myself as a victim of the individuals criticizing me. I had few communication skills about how I felt because I believed that suppressing and numbing my feelings was necessary to endure the pain I experienced. Therefore, emotional honesty was not even a possibility.

Enmeshed in perceiving myself as a victim, I communicated poorly or not at all, giving people harsh looks without explaining why I was upset, laughing at cruel jokes as though it was okay for me to bear the brunt of them, and pretending things were okay when I was deeply hurt. Loyal to the principles of a victim, I was hoping that if people saw I was unhappy, they would choose to treat me differently. Victimhood was slated to fail from the beginning. I didn't know that then.

I now know that I was deeply angry and blaming the individuals I created to criticize me. I mostly ignored or suppressed my feelings, creating distressing resentment whether I was aware of these feelings or not.

Since I had eliminated the natural process of dealing with and neutralizing negative emotions by feeling them, these toxic emotions built up, creating health challenges. More and more force was required to keep the blame, anger, and resentment suppressed as the unrelenting criticism from others continued.

Reaching middle age, I began to understand that the external criticism I experienced was a by-product of my own internal self-criticism. Every time I criticized myself, I set in motion someone in my external world criticizing me to show me that I was very critical to myself. Honestly, through the first thirty years of my life I didn't have a clue that is the way reality works.

Reality is created like a projector shining light on my inner film to create an image that defines my physical reality. The projector is really the light of God inside me. My inner film contains my behavior and my physical, emotional, and mental patterns. It creates an external image which is my reality or life. As with any film, the criticism on the reel projected the same criticism on the screen.

If I wanted the criticism to stop on the projected image which was my external reality, I had to remove the criticism from the film itself. It is the film that holds the patterns inside me which created both my internal and external criticism.

Trying to destroy the projected image through blame and fighting does nothing but destroy the external reality without making any change in the root cause of the problem—my inner film that contained the criticism patterns. If my inner film is modified or healed, then the image of reality will shift with it. If my inner film does not contain criticism, the projected external image will not have criticism in it. When you begin to really understand this, you have an enormous tool to begin shifting your reality to what you love. Until you do, you will tend to focus on fighting your external world, rather than creating positive change that can only come from an internal shift.

Once I realized this, I had the ability to walk out of my traps of internal and external criticism. By eliminating my self-criticism, I was also eliminating the external criticism I received from others.

Once I had this understanding, healing criticism became almost fun. When someone criticized me, I learned not to waste a second focusing on the other person. I learned that the cause of the criticism was inside me, and I had the ability to heal it. So when someone hurled abusive criticism, instead of resenting and blaming them, I would lavish love and praise on myself. What an amazing process with wondrous positive results! Steadily, I saw my world changing with less and less external criticism.

I put the healing of my self-criticism to the ultimate test recently. My family was uncomfortable about my career choice of teaching self-love. This saddened me because I love my teaching and the beautiful results the students achieve. When I thought I was ready, I sent my family a video of one of my TV shows. My heart wanted to share with them as hearts love to do; I also wanted to test how much self-criticism was left inside me. Some time went past without comment. I did not bring up the subject, uncertain whether the television show had upset them or they simply didn't want to watch it. One day when I was talking to my family, they mentioned that they had decided that the time had come to finally watch my video. I breathed deeply, preparing myself. I knew before sending the tape that I must be ready to deal with any of their responses and face the part of me that had created it. To my amazement there was not one negative comment. The focus of their response was centered more on the dress I wore and how I looked rather that the content. The comments were kind. I passed! I knew that I had mastered the self-critical part of me. With great self-love, I celebrated my long sought-after victory over my self-criticism.

Do you keep your focus on the individuals who criticize you with accompanying resentment, pain, and blame? . . 🌹 . . Or do you realize that they are holding a pointer to the self-criticism that is inside of you? . . 🌹 . . Are you open to taking responsibility for ending criticism of you? . . 🌹 . . Are you willing to stop criticizing yourself to free up external criticism?

You will love the results if you do. Once you begin to dissolve the patterns which create criticism, your life becomes more pleasant and relaxed. As you gain self-mastery in dissolving criticism from your reality, you heal pain that keeps your heart anxious and diminished. Great freedom and joy comes from this.

Easy Pearls of Wisdom

Pearl Thirteen

Lost Objects

Losing an object we need or love hurts. What a way to waste time and energy and create stress. Don't lose heart, there is a way out of being a victim to this!

Imagine the object as though it is still in your physical reality. I lost a piece of jewelry that I dearly loved. For months I couldn't bear the possibility of something that meant so much no longer being present in my world. So after having explored all possibilities, with nowhere else to look, I chose to act as though I had my jewelry.

I imagined placing the jewelry on my body and touched it as though it was physically on me. Every time I thought about it, I would physically touch where I wore it and express how much I loved this jewelry. After several hours, I went upstairs and sitting on top of my jewelry box was my lost jewelry.

I was convinced the jewelry had materialized out of nowhere. Later, my assistant mentioned that she had found my jewelry in a place she knew I hadn't thought of and had placed it on my jewelry chest. Had I not loved myself enough in this way, I would still be without my jewelry.

I also lost a very expensive bottle of essential rose oil. The loss of the oil felt harsh and hurt my feelings. I kept imagining that the bottle was in my hands and world. It did not reappear in a timely manner, so I bought another bottle. For Christmas, one of my students gave me a bottle of the same essential rose oil. The bottle must have been truly lost. My love for myself, which caused me to feel and express my love for my bottle of rose oil, caused another bottle to come to me as a gift. In the end, the universe returned an equivalent bottle to me. Not only did I get the extra bottle of rose oil, but I also was able to experience the feeling of God's love giving back what I had lost.

This powerful understanding takes us out of being victims of our world into being powerful creators. After these experiences, I tend to relax if something is missing because I know that I have the ability to bring it or something equivalent back into my world. Try this the next time you lose something you love. Once you have confidence that you are not a victim of losing what you love, you will find that you are much less likely to lose something you value.

Pearl Fourteen

Birthdays!

I love birthdays. I used to teach birthday workshops to help people enrich their lives and learn a wonderful way to love themselves. Loving myself on my birthday was not something I was born knowing how to do.

My parents gave me one birthday party as a child when I was six. My most vivid memory of this party was screaming in pain as a boy destroyed my new umbrella which I thought was so beautiful and special. I remember feeling devastated as the adults ran to discover why I was screaming. They grabbed the remains of my umbrella from the little boy and handed me the twisted and broken pieces. They told me not to be upset and cry. My broken umbrella told me it was unsafe to create what I love.

From the first grade until I completed my M.S. in biochemistry, I had final exams on my birthday. From that much test-taking and a blemished concept of a birthday party from my younger years, I learned to endure or forget my birthdays until I began focusing on self-love.

As self-love became a way of life, I noticed the rich opportunity I had to use this day as a focus of what I desired to create for the year. I began to carefully plan each of my birthdays to reflect the essence of the year I sought to create. For example, if my heart wanted the year to be rich with social interactions, I would create a social event or a birthday party on that day to give myself a boost towards creating it throughout the year. However, if my heart was desiring a quieter and more inward year, I would choose to spend my day alone or with a few close friends.

For several of my birthdays, God had an agenda that I simply flowed with. These were always special. For example, my son's high school graduation occurred on my birthday. I did not have to plan this birthday; God had already done it for me.

I had a breathtaking sacred experience that occurred on one of my birthdays in which I chose to plan nothing but to simply be available. Most of this day I spent in a state of deep connection to God that was truly beautiful and special. This year I felt strongly would be a year where I would simply allow God to lead without my conscious input. Unless the day is already created, such as my son's graduation or the year where I let God lead without conscious input, I carefully plan it by listening to my heart.

I have shared these teachings with my students. Observing them apply these principles has been very rewarding for me. Unless people have self-love training, they tend to do what others impose on them or nothing at all. When this occurs, sharing time on their birthday with others may come from guilt or obligation which prevents them from creating and experiencing what their hearts love. My students learn to carefully chose what they do on their birthday. Who they are with and what they create are carefully felt within their hearts before plans are made. My students have learned to simply not create others imposing themselves on them on their birthday. They have also learned to clearly ask others whom they desire to be with to be available to help them create what their hearts truly desire.

First, they plan the most ideal creation that their heart wants to experience for the actual day. This includes what they do, where they do it, and with whom. For the people who are special to them, but for whatever reason are not included in their birthday experience, they suggest getting together usually after their birthday. This works extremely well once an individual learns to clearly communicate what his or her heart truly desires. When others feel the sincerity of your heart, they usually love supporting what you are creating. If you do not want to be with someone, then it will hurt your heart if you use your mind to force yourself to endure or create something different than what you truly desire to please them.

It is wonderfully satisfying when you learn to create exactly what your heart desires to experience. First, you must learn that it is your birthright to experience what you love on your birthday. Knowing that this birthday experience will support you throughout the year to create what you love helps you to focus on what your heart truly desires to create. Second, you then learn how to communicate to others what you desire in a loving way that allows them to support what your heart desires. Creating birthdays you love brings a profound richness to your life and provides a focus on what you desire to create.

Have you learned to lovingly and clearly communicate what you desire for your birthday? . .❦. . Or does your tummy knot up when you desire to communicate your heart's desire to others? . .❦. . Are you willing to learn to love yourself by creating birthdays that deeply reflect what your heart desires to experience?

Learning to fully honor and create what you love on your birthday helps create a structure of this love flowing into your new year. There is a richness of acknowledging yourself as a creator of what you love on your birthday that supports you throughout your next birthday year. Don't miss this wonderful opportunity.

Pearl Fifteen

Computers and Me

I love computers and printers. I love how easily information can be transferred through them. However, my computers work only as well as I do, moment by moment. The minute I buy one, my computer takes on my mental and emotional nature.

If my heart is open, and I am feeling blessed and abundant, then my computer works perfectly. If my mind is harmonious, balanced, and stable, then so too is my computer. But alas, if I am struggling with difficult emotions or if my mind is spinning too fast with chaotic thoughts, then my computer perfectly creates a physical expression of my struggling mind and emotions. One day my computer operates at top efficiency helping me to create what I love, and the next day my computer rides my negative thoughts and emotions to provide a tangible experience of the frustration I feel.

I used to go crazy with my computer. I would storm around convinced the computer and printer were out to make my life impossible. "Lousy design! Low reliability! The miserable machine isn't working. I can't stand another moment of this computer. It's the computer's fault."

Suddenly, I had a tangible target for the tornado inside me that existed prior to sitting down in front of my computer. The truth was that it seldom had anything to do with the computer. I was upset before I touched my computer. Perhaps I understood why I was upset or perhaps not—in this situation, it made little difference. My whirlwind of negative thoughts and emotions were brewing a tornado, and I was determined to make the computer the bad guy.

I short-circuited several computers before I learned about the intimate bond that existed between me and my possessions. Once an item becomes mine, it is directly affected by my thoughts and feelings. When I maintain loving thoughts and feelings, my possessions are reliable and work well for me. If not, my thoughts and feelings create stress.

When my mind is peaceful and loving, my computer operates well. When I'm not loving, my computer throws an electrical fit much like my own mental-emotional tantrum. I have seen this so often in my world that I am convinced that scientists will demonstrate, if they have not already done so, that sensitive electrical circuits such as those that exist in computers are affected by the electromagnetic nature of our minds and emotions.

When I have computer problems now, which is extremely rare, I usually get up and deal with my thoughts and emotions. If I sense that I am feeling chaotic, impatient, or frustrated, then I remove myself from my computer to protect it from the sparking and spewing that is going on inside my mind and with my emotions. I often will turn the computer off and start it again when I am peaceful. This works very well for me. I no longer feel victimized by my computer. I know if I protect my computer from me when I am off-balanced, then my computer works well for me the rest of the time.

This principle applies to our cars, home maintenance, or any other inanimate objects that share the same atomic nature that we do. Once we realize that our thoughts and feelings give off electromagnetic signals that can create stress for inanimate objects, this understanding provides the opportunity to walk away from being a victim of these objects. We can learn to provide positive influences so these objects support us in a harmonious way.

As you begin to observe this phenomenon, you will be amazed at the correlation you uncover between your peace and the peace within your physical world. Observe how stress in your thoughts and emotions affects your possessions, animals, or relationships.

Once you start seeing these correlations you gain a valuable tool to create a peaceful, harmonious reality, free from destructive influence. Until you do, you won't understand that your frustrated thoughts and emotions are the culprits wreaking havoc in your physical world. When you get it, then you have the opportunity to shift your reality to support you, rather than work against you.

Pearl Sixteen

It's My Life, So I'll Write Contracts I Love

I believe that we create every aspect of our lives. We think we are victims until we learn this. Sometimes, we are aware of what we create. However, many things we experience are created on subtle levels we are not aware of. Either way, it is our life, and we have the divine right to create what we love. When our lives are focused on creating what our hearts love, we feel good and the consequences are good for everyone.

However, we are on a planet governed by free will, so we also have the right to create what we hate. When we create based on fear and hate, we hurt ourselves and others.

A teenager named Tina asked to have a session with me. She explained that she was terrified of flying in airplanes, and it was causing her tremendous stress. I explained to her that she had the right to live what she wanted to live. I asked her if she wanted to be terrorized by flying. Her response was, "Definitely not." I asked her if she would like to love flying and have wonderful experiences at the airport, while she was flying, and after she left the plane. She made a humming sound as people often do when they feel their heart. "That would be wonderful. But how?" she asked.

I told her to write a contract between herself and God. I suggested that in her contract she clearly explain to God exactly how she wanted to experience everything associated with flying: planes, airports, and flying itself. Then I told her to read her contract to herself and God every night for three nights.

After she finished this, I explained this contract would exist between her and God for the rest of her life. Because of this, she would never have to fear air travel again. I assured her that God would receive her contract and help her create it. Much to her amazement, she recently reported that she flew home free of fear.

We create our lives. It is our choice whether we allow God to help us create what we love, or we create ourselves as victims of God and man. Are you living with fear in areas of your life that create stress for you? . . . Are you open to writing a new contract between you and God to make your life more comfortable, confident, and loving?

If so, it is your divine right to create new contracts that allow God to greatly bless and comfort you. It is also your divine right to tear up and dissolve old contracts that are based on fear and victimization which scare and hurt you.

Pearl Seventeen

Feeding My Home With Love

Have you ever compared the feelings you get when you walk into different homes? Where there is love, the home is warm and together. You relax immediately, open your heart, and enjoy the space that has been fed love. One of my grandmothers loved her home. Her home was a creation of beauty. The aroma of rich and abundant foods filled with love were always there to support a pleasant and long visit. Although we didn't verbally communicate much because I was young, she often rubbed my back, and I knew she loved me. People loved to visit her. Her space was inviting and fed daily with love.

On the other hand, what about homes where there is only anger, unkind words, and the absence of love? My other grandmother created such a space. My body would cringe when we went to visit her. I could smell the negativity before I entered the door, and it hurt me. She did not feed her space with love. With the absence of love, her cooking was uninviting and infused with drudgery and spite for having been forced to do something she disliked. I wanted to leave her space as soon as possible.

Has it ever occurred to you that unless you feed a space with love, it deteriorates? Look at abandoned buildings and homes. They deteriorate if there is not love present. It doesn't matter how much was spent on the building materials. If a space is not fed love, it will deteriorate. The instant that someone chooses to feed an abandoned building love, suddenly the space begins to recover.

You might say, "But they deteriorate because no one is maintaining them." That is the aftermath of no love. An abandoned building without love goes quickly, especially when there has been hatred and rage involved, such as harsh divorces, lawsuits, or bankruptcy. These buildings decline much faster than the building materials warrant. Observe this. You will be surprised at the correlations you see.

Go into a home where there is expressed violence and rage. Things break more quickly and deteriorate faster. You might say, "Well, that's obvious. The people probably get angry and knock things around. That's why it deteriorates faster." If they are physically violent, this is part of it. But what if they are verbally violent? This will also create a general deterioration of everything. The plumbing breaks often, blinds and drapes fall apart, and appliances require extra effort to maintain. In an emotionally and mentally violent home, rage and hate create destruction. There simply isn't enough love to keep the space from deteriorating and losing the cohesion that holds everything together. Love provides the cohesion.

As I was exploring this, I visited a wealthy friend who owns several large homes. Even though he spends only a short amount of the year in the home I was visiting, I saw how he keeps love focused to maintain this beautiful mansion. He loves this home and was expressive about his love for it. His love for it touched my heart and reminded me of the open love a child has for a special treasure.

His heart naturally understood that this beautiful home must have love to stay alive and full. He has a caretaker who knows how to love spaces too—this is no accident. While there, I overheard his caretaker and him going over minute details about the home, which surprised me that he would place so much focus and attention there. He has several businesses worldwide, yet these details had his full attention and love. He cared about these details, and by caring, he kept love present. He knew how to keep his beautiful creation rich with love. I felt it when I entered.

You might say, "Well, it is easy for the rich man to maintain his home. He has the wealth to do this." My reply is that I agree that he had monetary wealth easily available to him, but it was his wealth of love and ability to love that kept his home beautiful and warm. Loving his home was not an obligation or duty in his mind, but rather a natural state of his heart. He consistently made choices that supported love and caring of his space. That was his heart's choice. The same heart choices of loving and caring for your space are available to you regardless of your financial situation. When you do make these heart choices, it transforms you and your spaces into love.

I am convinced that if a person, who felt they had no ability to fix a deteriorating space, would love themselves and the space enough, then their love would restructure their space. This restructuring might take different forms such as someone volunteering to help, a renewed avail-ability of energy that supported the home coming together, or whatever. Love is very powerful and provides solutions to problems that otherwise might appear impossible.

Do you love your home? . . 🌹. . Or do you withhold love from it? . . 🌹. . Are you willing to love your home regardless of any reasons that your mind tells you that you should withhold love from it?

Feeding your home with love makes all the difference, not only to your home, but to the quality of the life you live in your home.

Pearl Eighteen

Taking the Resistance Out of Exercise— Putting the Reward In

Exercise has tended to be an area of my life where resistance, rebellion, and giving up usually won. I once bought an exercise machine. Before the clerk could get it into my car, I was already rebelling and creating rules on how it—the machine—could not force me to do what I didn't want to do. I knew then that my future with the machine was clouded.

Not to my surprise, I could force myself to do exercise for only a short while, and then the resistance would get so big that any excuse was more than adequate to justify not exercising. Soon, I was in total resistance and stopped exercising. I kept the machine, thinking that I might use it one day, if the resistance diminished. My self-love work would not allow me to force myself, as I had in the past, to do something I had so much resistance against. So this stalemate continued for years.

One day I sensed that my body was closed off to receiving the wealth that I deserved and desired. I felt that my body was too ungrounded for me to properly focus on creating wealth. Suddenly, I could sense that if I did three yoga sun salutations a day and eleven minutes on the machine, this would help my body to be more physical, and that would directly benefit my finances. If I did these exercises eleven minutes the first thing in the morning, it would open my body to receiving financial empowerment all day.

With this perception, I transitioned from willfully resisting exercise to loving to do it. And I especially loved that it required only eleven minutes. Initially, what I enjoyed was the sense that the exercise would help me feel more present, which allowed me to connect more easily to my financial desires. As I did, I began to love the exercise as well as its impact on my body. As I look back on this mental shift, I realize that what I really did was to find a link between my exercise and something I desired. I loved this desire enough that it helped me to move through my resistance to exercise.

It was amazing what happened. I exercise every day and love doing it. I feel really good about it and am enjoying the physical strength and agility that I now have. My body and physical awareness are much more present and focused throughout the day on sharing knowledge, which is an important way for me to create financial success. I have recommended to my students that they find a link between something they resist and something they desire to help transition out of resistance in an area of their life. They have reported similar positive responses.

I was at a party where a student commented on how athletic my legs were. This tickled my heart. A few years ago, that would have been an impossible comment to receive. Once she said this, several of my other students who had heard my story replied at the same time, "Eleven minutes a day—not twelve—only eleven." We all laughed as I explained how much I loved that I only asked myself to do eleven minutes of exercises a day.

Increased wealth is not the motivation for everyone. I have a student whose heart desired more friends. Rather than seeking financial success as a motivation, she used exercise as a way to focus on creating more friends. This is a wonderful way to assist our bodies by increasing strength and agility and improving our health while we create what we love.

Does your heart guide you to exercise? . .🌹. . Or do you use your will to force yourself to do something you do not desire to do? . .🌹. . What is a motivation that will allow your heart to support you in exercising? . .🌹. . How many minutes are you willing to go without creating resistance? . .🌹. . From this pearl of wisdom, do you understand how to use something that you love and value to help you move forward in an area of your life where you are stuck and in resistance?

Exercise is a choice. When you use your heart to find something about exercise that you truly love, you create a powerful tool to gently shift yourself out of resistance to exercise. A great way to love yourself!

Pearl Nineteen

In A Bind—How to Hang Onto My Integrity

A long time ago, I was in a car accident. The car repair took longer than the allotted time my insurance company would pay for a rental car. They suggested that I purchase a car for a few thousand dollars and then sell it once my car was fixed. In a state of pain and victimization from my accident, I chose the first car I saw in the paper. I purchased this car for several thousand dollars, and then it stopped working after a few days!

How could I get my money back when I had purchased a lemon? Someone suggested that I use the same tricks that the unscrupulous person used who sold it to me; make it look like it ran when it didn't. I couldn't do that to someone else—too mean. I honestly did not want to hurt someone else like that person hurt me. So I created in my mind a clear desire to find a buyer who knew exactly what they were buying and would purchase it anyway. That way, they would not get hurt like I did.

I advertised the car in the paper. A potential buyer saw the car in the driveway before knocking on my door. He walked into my home, and the first thing he said was, "This car is a piece of junk! It has the following things wrong with it." His list went on for at least fifteen items, which, by the way, were all true. "My business is to take pieces of junk like this and restore them." My heart laughed. He told me everything I wanted to hear so that I knew he was not in any way victimized by his purchase, as I had been. It cost me several hundred dollars to get a wise buyer. For that several hundred dollars, I got a huge laugh, kept my integrity, and saw my ability to create exactly what I was asking for. I knew it was worth it!

The man who sold the lemon to me had not learned how to keep his integrity. Perhaps he laughed at what he did to me, but his laugh was covering his meanness and darkness which always ultimately creates pain and suffering. I always choose integrity in my life.

Have you given away some of your integrity because you did not know how to meet your needs and keep your integrity at the same time? . .❦. . Feel if you could have used what you learned here to get your needs met while keeping your integrity. Is there an area in your life now where your integrity is in jeopardy? . .❦. . How can you keep your integrity and move your life forward at the same time?

We literally create every nuance of our lives. When we shift our creative desires to integrity and mutual benefit for ourselves and others, we facilitate our lives shifting to patterns of goodness and love. Feel how much peace this would bring you.

Pearl Twenty

What Did You Do to My Cat?

The second workshop that I taught many years ago was at a friend's beautiful home. He had graciously agreed to leave for the duration of the women's workshop. After meeting this group of women interested in love—his "payoff" for sharing his home—he made one parting comment as he walked out the door: "My son's cat is here, but it never leaves the back bedroom. By the way, Lucky hates women," he yelled as the door closed.

As soon as he left and the workshop began, the "woman-hating cat" Lucky walked into the living room and methodically touched each woman. The cat never left the workshop and obviously felt comfortable and connected. I forgot to mention to my friend this strange behavior for a woman-hating cat who never left the back bedroom.

A week later I saw him at a store. Upset, he said, "What did you do to my cat?" I got a little uncomfortable as I scanned my memory for anything that might have hurt or upset the cat. I couldn't remember anything. Unsure, I apologetically replied, "Nothing that I am aware of. Lucky stayed with us throughout the day, connected with everyone, and appeared to enjoy himself."

"That's what I'm talking about," he replied. "It's my son's cat. I could live with it when it stayed alone in the back room and hated women. Now it never goes back to that room and wants to connect with everyone. You've turned it into one of those touchy-feely animals who loves women. What am I going to do with it now?" he asked with a smile on his face. I didn't have an answer for him.

Love affects animals as powerfully as it does us. Our pets take on our characteristics. I did not have to tune in to my friend's son to have a good idea what emotional baggage his son was carrying. Lucky was in isolation and pain as a result of it. The love offered by the women in our workshop was simply too inviting. The cat chose not to continue to merge with and hold loyal to the hatred for women and isolated feelings that he had learned and experienced while with my friend's son. The cat chose love and freed himself to express his true nature of love. I hope that my friend's son eventually did the same.

After the powerful transformation this cat made, I clearly understood that the self-love work I was doing affects the animals as much as it does people. Because of the release of deep, painful emotions during the workshop, there was concern about allowing sensitive animals in my workshops. Eventually, I learned to trust the choices of the animals, the same as I trusted the choices of the humans who came to my workshops.

I explained to the people who hosted workshops in their homes that some of the animals would choose love and some would not. From the frequent feedback we received from the pet owners, animals who made the choice of self-love frequently made profound shifts after the workshop in terms of how comfortable, warm, and healthy they were.

Have you noticed that your animals are a reflection of you and your families' personality and characteristics? . . . . Do you understand that your stress can cause problems within your animals? . . . . Are you patient with your animals if you are going through a difficult time?

As you realize that your animals are a reflection of the best and also most uncomfortable parts of you, you have an important tool to assist in dealing with difficult animals. If you change the imbalances in you that your animals are showing to you, you free both yourself and your animals of the stress. What a loving way to bring harmony to yourself and your animals.

Pearl Twenty-One

Speeding Tickets No More!

I realize only now that I was very angry in the midst of my divorce many years ago which means I was very hurt. At that time in my life, I was much better at giving other people advice about their emotions than I was about dealing with my own. Mostly, I was numb, even when I was very, very angry and hurt.

My former husband did something associated with cars during the divorce that upset me. Because I did not have any idea how to deal with my emotions or to communicate in an effective manner, I transformed my frustration into getting speeding tickets—one after another. Suddenly, I went from never having any tickets to having too many of them.

I created the opportunity to become somewhat aware of my hidden anger through attending three arduous four-hour driving classes designed to bore speeding motorists into slowing down. After the third class, I knew I had to deal with the situation.

Eventually, I was able to feel how angry I was at my former husband and became aware of the situation that had caused me to transfer this anger over to getting speeding tickets. I released the anger as best as I knew how. After this, I was pulled over one more time. Instead of getting a speeding ticket, I was given only a warning by the policeman. Yeah! I knew I had broken the cycle.

After seeing how vulnerable I was to my emotions, most of which I was not even aware of, I felt that I needed greater protection for myself in terms of accidents, car safety, and tickets.

I had been studying sacred symbols and their ability to focus and shift awareness. After I created so many speeding tickets, I wanted a focus to keep my thoughts and emotions on safety and freedom from disruptions. So I created this process, described below, to focus my mind and heart on creating a safe driving experience. I do my safety exercise each time I get ready to start my car.

Safety Exercise

The exercise is done by moving the hands up and down in specific places in front of you to symbolize the following directions: 1) front, 2) right, 3) back, 4) left, 5) above, 6) below, and 7) within (center).

1. With thumb on top, resting on fingers, point the right hand straight out in front of you. Left-handed people would reverse this.

2. For each direction, you will move the hand up and down four times, with about a six inch range from top to bottom.

3. Do the movements in a three-dimensional diamond pattern beginning at the front (1) of the body, about 18 inches away from the solar plexus. Do the up-and-down pattern, then move to the right (2) and do the same, then to the back (3) position (about six inches in front of the solar plexus), then to the left (4), to the above (5) position (about 10 inches away from the eyes), to the below (6) position (about 10 inches away from the belly), and finally to the center (7) position (about 10 inches away from the solar plexus).

4. As your hand moves up-down, down-up four times in each of these positions, it creates an in-the-air pattern of two pyramids that have the same base—the square-diamond.

5. This perfected pattern of wholeness is a symbol that helps us focus on balance, harmony, and attentiveness to experience life as love.

Using this exercise has helped me to instinctively slow down a few miles before I see a police car with radar, avoiding going over the speed limit, and my car has been amazingly reliable and maintenance-free. I have had no speeding tickets in over fourteen years. When I do the symbol, I know that I am actually creating protection for myself and my car. I feel as though I am feeding my car with love and balance to prevent it from aging or having mechanical problems. I love having this extra sense of protection and the focus to support my car and my well-being. I know that I am creating a safe reality on the road.

The focus brought by this symbol allows me to center myself into a harmonious state of balance. By creating harmony within myself, disharmony, such as tickets and road problems, does not get created.

Is there an area of your life where you use anger and hurt to create stress and problems in your life? . . 🌹 . . Are you willing to look deep inside to feel the cause of disruptions in your life? . . 🌹 . . Are you willing to create a focus, whether it be a symbol, quiet time, or a warm bath, that assists you in creating a sense of peace and harmony within yourself?

As you learn to do this, in truth you take responsibility for mastering yourself and your life. Don't delay learning how to create peace and safety in your world.

Pearl Twenty-Two

Is Running Out of Gasoline My Best Choice?

One evening while on a long trip, I noticed that my car's gasoline level was lower than I normally allow it to get. I began to get anxious to find a gas station. My concern about running out of gas quickly became reality as my car began sputtering and losing power. I slowly pulled to the side of the road. It was late at night, and I sensed that the next station was way too far away for a simple solution.

After trying to restart my car enough times to determine that there was no hope, I sat there evaluating my options. The first option was to flag someone down (despite the potential dangers), go to a station, and have them return me to my car with gasoline. I figured that this would probably take well over an hour and involve a lot of drama. As I explored other options, such as asking someone to transfer their fuel into my car, I had concerns of even more drama. I didn't give up thinking about ways to refuel my car. I was not particularly upset, but I knew I wanted a good plan before I took action.

I desired to eliminate the drama and the wasted hour or so of frustration. Suddenly I knew the solution—attempt to start the car one more time. The difference this time was that my heart was clear that I wanted my car to start. So with confidence that although I had explored multiple possibilities of drama and trauma, I simply wasn't interested in them. I turned the key, and the car started as though there had never been a problem. I drove to the next station and learned a lot about my ability to create whatever my heart desired.

Have you ever taken the path of frustration and trauma rather than simply creating something to support you? . . . . . Do you know how to calm yourself and lovingly support life working for you? . . . . . Or do you use the trauma to give you an outlet for your negative emotions and validation of being a victim of your reality? . . . . . Are you open to creating a more harmonious life?

When stress enters your life, learn to relax and calmly consider alternatives. Get very clear what you want to create, versus what you may perceive is possible or not possible. Then calmly create what your heart desires.

Pearl Twenty-Three

Am I Your Teacher?

I am a teacher to the core of my being. As I collected more and more knowledge to assist individuals, I naturally wanted to pass it along. Although I have many people wanting to study with me, I had a desire to share my knowledge with my family. When listening to them, I would blurt out the kind of advice that my students would ask me for. Consistently, my family would recoil and make it obvious that they did not value or have any use for it. I had worked for years on healing the part of me that would create this.

My sister taught me a wonderful lesson I would like to share with you. One day, she was talking about her relationship with our parents. My sister said that she would rather do without or not understand something that might potentially limit or hurt her than have them tell her how to do it. She clearly expressed how important it was for her to figure it out by herself regardless of the cost to herself.

I finally got it. I realized that my family simply did not choose me as their teacher. At last, I deeply accepted and understood that it is their privilege whom they choose and whom they don't choose to teach them. I was violating their selection. As a result, I was wasting my energy which could more appropriately be given to those who did choose me as their teacher. In addition, my unsolicited and unwanted teaching caused stress for them and me.

Since then, I carefully observe whether or not I am someone's teacher. If

I am, then that person carries a different level of respect for me. If I am not someone's teacher, then that person, like my family, chooses not to desire or value my advice. This allows me to relax rather than focus on helping the person.

If someone does not choose me as his or her teacher, then it does not mean that the person does not love me. It simply means that this person has chosen to relate to me in another way. I now love the variety this adds to my life. It also allows me to rest and play.

Observe carefully who has chosen you as their teacher and who has not. You will know they have by the respect and value they give to your teaching. Share with those who have chosen you. The others may want the freedom to love you without you focusing on how to help them. They, like my sister, may have a deep desire to figure it out for themselves. This understanding has definitely made my life smoother, easier, and more fulfilling.

Do you have a compulsive desire to teach someone who does not want to learn from you? . . ❧ . . Family members are often the ones who can pull us into this uncomfortable waste of our energy. What causes you to override their desire to do it their way? . . ❧ . . Are you ready to let this go entirely, respecting their desire to choose their own teacher? . . ❧ . . Are you willing to transfer the focus and energy you placed on them instead to support your own self-love and others who love, respect, and value your teachings?

There is great freedom when you do.

Feeding My Heart

Pearl Twenty-Four

Creating Time to Value My Heart

We live in a fast-paced society. The quiet and peaceful time our hearts need tends to be postponed and relegated to something we do either when we don't have anything else left to do or when we reach complete exhaustion.

Our hearts are the key to fulfillment. Unfortunately, we can seduce ourselves into working more, which leads to less fulfillment. In truth, this is a self-inflicted, brutal cycle that hurts. This oppression makes us perceive that we can gain wealth, prestige, and fulfillment by working harder and harder. In order to handle the pain of this survival pattern that blocks our hearts, we are driven to addictions that numb us from feeling and that create self-destructive escapes which only increase the problems.

As we drive more toward doing rather than living, our minds create their own validations and excuses to not give our hearts the necessary time to create fulfillment, peace, and joy. They tell the heart, "When I retire, then I can create what I love. When my children get older . . . when I get my bills paid . . . when I get the new job or new house . . . when I lose weight. When . . . when . . . when!"

After years of this, our hearts tend to give up because they cannot trust that we will give them the necessary time to feel and experience what our hearts love. This denial of our hearts may be deadly, causing us to build up so much pain that we create accidents, addictions, and diseases to escape.

In order for you to create time for your heart, you must first value your heart. Do you? . . ❧ . . Do you truly value sitting under a tree, holding hands, and being with someone you love, with no list or agenda of what to do or not do? . . ❧ . . You will know if you do truly value your heart, because only then will you create time to experience what your heart values.

Do you value rest, pleasure, and play as much as you value work and activity? . . ❧ . . If you do, then rest, pleasure, and play will have great importance in your life, and you will create time for it. So often, these are used as a tool to keep us going once exhaustion has set in. In others words, if we can't handle life anymore, then rest, pleasure, and play are pulled out as last-resort tools to use for survival when we have pushed ourselves way past depletion.

Do you promise your heart time, and then quickly undercut the promise once delivery is near? . . ❧ . . If you do, then each time you hurt your heart in this way you instill deeper distrust of your heart for your mind. Your heart would not take rest, pleasure, and play from you. Yet your mind may aggressively withhold these with desperate justification.

Unless your mind is programmed to support your heart, it can deny heart pleasure while it thinks that it is doing you a favor and supporting your best interest. The more your mind creates this, the less your heart feels respected and valued. As this painful pattern continues, eventually your heart will close and give up. When this occurs, experiencing the joys of life becomes difficult or impossible, and your mind has full reign to drive you into more abuse. This pattern creates common stress-related syndromes that can have serious repercussions on your health.

For someone with a healthy heart, creating time for his or her heart is a moment-by-moment choice. The person's heart is given time to feel throughout each day, rather than having to wait until retirement when the person won't have anything better to do. A healthy heart creates the opportunity to love at work, at home, and anywhere it is throughout the day.

Do you create time for your heart? If you feel that you do not have time to spare, then create the time. Walk a little slower as you go to the bathroom at work and open your heart to the people you see on the way. As you wait for the copy machine or your children, as you cook, or as you drive, open your heart and feel love for yourself and those you love. It won't take any additional time, and it will allow you to begin experiencing love for yourself.

Love yourself enough to create time to feel what your heart loves to experience and then lavish it upon yourself. When your mind understands how much you value heart time, it can learn to support you in creating it. You have taken a giant step toward self-love when your mind provides time for your heart. You will be amazed to realize that once you do value and choose to create this time, ample time for heart pleasures suddenly appears. Without heart time, you risk missing out and not truly showing up for your life. With heart time, you create the best that life has to offer!

Pearl Twenty-Five

Valuing My Heart

My heart loves china and its beauty. Once I got married, my china symbolized love, friends, and luxury. The beautiful parties I created with my china were blessings of sharing, joy, and play for me. I felt enormous amounts of love when I gave a party and knew that everyone felt the warmth and was blessed by it.

When I began focusing on my spiritual work about twenty years ago, my mind told me that spiritual people didn't do that kind of thing and that I had more important ways to spend my time. This arrogant decision crushed my heart. At that time in my life, my parties were the freest way I knew to open my heart so wide that I could truly share myself and my love with others. As the rules of my spiritual path became more clearly defined, I discarded my china as unimportant and insignificant. I had no understanding at that time that my true spiritual path was bringing God's love into my heart and my daily life.

So I discarded my china and social life which had been such a joy to me. When I would walk through a department store, my longing heart would try to sneak a peak at the china. My spiritual self, which was rather stranded in my mind at that time, pulled my head away and explained to me that china was unimportant. My heart would wince from the sense of loss.

At that time I did not understand self-love and how cruel my mind was being to my heart. My heart had no understanding of its value to my spirituality and mind. Had it known its true value, it would have said, "Stop it, mind. You have only part of the picture, and you are hurting me." Then my heart would have asked my mind to feel the china at the department store. My heart would have burst open and reminded my mind how much we loved china. It would have touched the beautiful plates and smiled with delight at the tiny little raised areas which create such a feeling of elegance. The amazing colors and shapes would have brought me joy.

My heart would have reminded my mind of how many people I loved through my parties where my china was used. My heart would have explained how important feeling love is, and without expressing that love, my life was empty and plain. If my heart had realized how important it was to me, it would have taught my mind to support it in creating what opened my heart.

Only many years later did my heart learn its value. Once it did, my heart taught my mind to value it, too. Once that occurred, beautiful china returned to my life to bless my heart and life with joy.

Have you used your mind to take away what your heart loves and values? . . ❧ . . If so, then perhaps restructuring your world to create what you love is in order. Until you teach your mind the value of your heart, your mind may have little interest in what your heart loves, often because it can't feel the importance. This creates pain in our physical world. Your heart may not understand how important it is to your fulfillment and well-being. Only when your heart understands how valuable it is can your mind be trained to support your heart.

What does your heart love? . . ❧ . . Notice the warm feelings that are created by simply remembering the items and activities that your heart enjoys. As you matured and your life got more complex, did you forget to give yourself these heart-supporting, heart-nurturing gifts?

Often these special things you love, you loved as a child. Their presence in your life helps to keep your inner child happy and alive. Have you forgotten them or made them unimportant in your daily life? . . ❧ . . In doing so, has that created sadness and loss for the inner child within your heart? . . ❧ . . What would your heart love for you to give to yourself that you have not allowed? . . ❧ . . Do you love yourself enough to bring this special feeling back into your life?

When you do allow the things your heart enjoys into your life, you allow your heart and inner child to feel valued and loved. Tremendous blessings unlock with creating your heart's delight.

Pearl Twenty-Six

Feeding My Heart

I f you seek a healthy heart, you must feed it much as you support your body with food. A healthy heart requires patience, nurturing, rest, affection, safety, peace, feeling valuable, gratefulness, and play to maintain itself. How do you feed your heart to keep it healthy?

It is usually easy to recognize individuals who are starving their hearts. They tend to be nervous and high strung, move very fast, have tight and drawn faces, and are tired and burdened-looking.

These people have withdrawn into their minds and have refused to feed their hearts. Most of their focus is usually centered in their minds, which are stressed and pushed too far. Their minds become like demanding drill sergeants who are out of touch with their hearts' needs, pushing their physical bodies beyond what both their hearts and bodies can sustain. If they persist long enough, stubbornly refusing to feed their hearts, life-threatening, stress-related diseases are the only things that will stop them.

My fifty-four-year-old dad had what would have been a fatal heart attack, had he not checked into a coronary care facility a few hours before. He did hard, demanding work in the company he owned and was involved in a lawsuit at that time. For many months he could think of nothing else other than the lawsuit, as the demands of his physically difficult job piled up.

His heart attack changed all of this and instantly pulled him from a job that hurt him. Unfortunately, his health was seriously and permanently jeopardized. If you were to ask him today about the lawsuit that contributed to his heart attack, he might have trouble remembering the details. It was so insignificant in the overall scheme of things once my dad had the heart attack, I don't even remember whether his company won or lost it. The only relevant thing about that lawsuit was that he used it to damage his body so he would end a career that was stressful and abusive to him.

My father simply did not know how to listen to his heart, which would have said, "You're tired and stressed, and the job hurts you. This job gives you no time to feed your heart. Quit and create what you love."

Prior to the heart attack, I am certain that if anyone had suggested that he quit his job because it was too stressful for him, he would have gotten very angry. Then he would have said, "But I have no choice. I have to work at this job to make a living. I have a fourteen-year-old child at home." After the heart attack, everything fell into place, and my father no longer had to work for money. His health was jeopardized so he could do small things to keep himself entertained, but there was no longer a focus on making money. If he had listened to his heart, he could have quit when the stress began to build and could have created a new career that gave his heart value. He could have retained his health and avoided frequent physical suffering for the rest of his life.

These teachings help individuals write a different script than what my dad knew how to write. I teach people how to hear and listen to their hearts. I help individuals generate enough self-love that they move themselves out of situations that hurt their hearts and force themselves to do things that damage and stress their bodies. Once they create enough self-love, everything supports feeding their hearts through time, patience, nurturing, rest, affection, safety, peace, feeling valuable, gratefulness, and play. With enough self-love, everything will be all right.

Have you structured your life to support your heart? . . . I can promise you that with enough self-love, any stressful situation can be uplifted. Where in your life is there stress that hurts and causes you to lock up your heart? . . . Are you open to creating changes in your life so that you may feed your heart?

These changes must start with you learning to love yourself. As you do, shifts occur which allow you to live what you love regardless of how impossible that may appear before you began to love yourself. The time is now to begin learning to love yourself.

Pearl Twenty-Seven

Allowing Myself to Receive Exactly What I Want

I love to sip hot water with limes. Once, I ordered limes for my hot water and the waitress returned, explaining that they were out of limes, but she sent someone to the store to get them for me. Instead of basking in the support of a restaurant providing exactly what I desired, I immediately back-peddled, telling the waitress that I would use lemon instead and that I did not feel good about them going to the store to provide what I had requested.

The waitress insisted that they wanted to provide exactly what I desired, and she would shortly return with my limes. As she walked away, I was shocked at my response. I experienced negative and uncomfortable feelings of regret that they were expending energy to provide what I desired. I was aghast at how insistent I was to assure that my desires were not supported by the energy and efforts of others.

With this much refusal to allow others to support me, I was working against my own heart's desire to feel supported and provided for. I immediately went inside myself to increase my self-love to a level of acceptance of others providing what I love, rather than working against them.

Although the lack of limes appeared to be a rather insignificant creation, this showed me how little I was willing to allow others to create what I love. The same patterns that did not want others to expend energy to create limes would affect creations in which I deeply wanted others to support me. Until these patterns were healed, I would create resistance and refuse to allow others to provide what I desired. I was unaware until this incident that I had these subconscious patterns working against my creative self. With these patterns revealed, I could use self-love and self-mastery to change these patterns from unsupportive to supportive.

Do you allow others to support you? . .✿. . Or do you shut them down with insistence that you are not worthy of their effort and desire to please you? . .✿. . Do you realize that these patterns of unworthiness prevent you from creating exactly what your heart loves? . .✿. . Also, these self-denying patterns assure that you never receive the support that blesses and pleases your heart.

Do you resist or push away the help of others? . .✿. . Or do you allow your heart to feel profoundly grateful that others are there to support your heart's desires?

If receiving from others is difficult for you, this is a red flag that more self-love is required. Choose to create and live what you love by increasing your love for yourself. When what you ask for and desire is offered to you, love what you have created.

Pearl Twenty-Eight

The Chemistry of Love

What we feel creates a chemical experience in our bodies. Studies with endorphins and other such chemicals have shown that certain activities create chemicals that can cause us to experience certain feelings. When we love, we create chemicals that enable us to experience goodness and well-being so that everything functions well within our bodies and in our creative world. The more we sustain these positive body chemicals, the better our world works.

It is important to focus on learning to sustain the chemistry of self-love in our bodies. We can use our love for other people, animals, or things outside of ourselves to evoke the chemistry of love. This is greatly beneficial.

However, until one addresses the beliefs that deal with self-love, there may exist patterns of separation, guilt, and hatred of self that continue to harm an individual. Address patterns that cause you to avoid loving yourself. I feel this is where the ultimate problem and ultimate solution lie for fulfillment. For many of us, *self-love must be learned,* because beliefs in our society, families, and religious training may say that loving self is bad or should be avoided. The good news is that it can be learned!

Since love is experienced through the chemistry of our bodies, how can we shift our chemistry away from toxic chemistry that causes us to feel bad about ourselves to a chemistry that brings well-being into our world? In my teachings, we use mirror work. If you are unfamiliar with mirror work, I suggest the book *You Can Heal Your Life* by Louise Hay[1].

I have students acquire mirrors approximately two feet by five feet at discount stores so that they can see their full bodies as they focus on loving themselves. It is not unusual for students to resist and hate themselves and the mirrors, until they begin creating a momentum of love as they say, "I love you," regardless of how difficult it is for them. Eventually, they will begin to feel such rich feelings about themselves that their time with their mirrors becomes an important aspect of their lives. As they do, the chemistry of the cells in their bodies shifts from denying love to living love. That makes all the difference in the quality of life they live.

Self-love must be maintained. My students discover that once their lives begin feeling abundant, warm, and loving, it is very easy to stop their mirror sessions. Based on my students' experience, they can ride the momentum they create for about eight days without noticing a difference. Then, if they avoid their self-love mirror sessions much past this, the momentum and consequently the quality of their lives diminish. Once they choose to return to their mirror work, it will take about another eight days to rebuild the momentum so that they begin feeling good again and their lives work well.

I do not know if mirror work is necessary throughout an individual's life in order to sustain self-love. However, the dedication to self-love is essential as long as an individual desires it. Part of the reason that it requires so much focus is that there are so many physical, emotional, and mental patterns that work against self-love.

Can you tell yourself that you love yourself in front of a mirror and experience a tangible feeling of love for yourself? . . ❧ . . Or is this an uncomfortable possibility that you resist and feel you would never want to give to yourself?

Does your body maintain a chemistry of self-love which supports your feeling safe, abundant, and blessed? . . ❧ . . If not, then are you willing to devote time to focus on creating a chemistry within your body that supports self-love?

Are you willing to take responsibility for creating the chemistry of love in your body? . . ❧ . . Or do you push and criticize yourself to assure that the chemistry of love is not allowed to bless your body? . . ❧ . . Do you know how to shift from the chemistry of the absence of love to the chemistry of love? . . ❧ . . Are you open to keeping the chemistry of love in your body throughout the day?

The chemistry of self-love feels good in your body. These good feelings invoke a positive chemistry that allows your life to work well. Creating this beneficial chemistry is your responsibility and also your birthright. Start now to increase your self-love to support the chemistry of self-love in your body.

[1]Louise L. Hay, *You Can Heal Your Life,* (1999), Hay House.

Pearl Twenty-Nine

An Open Heart for Men

When my teachings began, the school focused on going the extra mile to encourage men to empower their hearts. The school's teachings made it very clear from the beginning that I had no interest or ability to teach men how to be men. My focus was on teaching men the principles of self-love and trusting that they would integrate and create a template of being a man of love from their understanding of living an open heart.

Before the school was ready to teach the first men's workshop, a survey of the men I knew was conducted to get their feelings about a workshop to awaken and empower men's hearts. When I asked one of my students about a workshop for men, he got so upset that I desired to teach men about love that he had to use his session time with me releasing his stress about the subject. He assured me that men didn't want that kind of thing and that homophobic issues were so strong that it would cause men to stay away. He was positive that men did not want to learn about their heart, and it was not safe.

I'm so glad I taught about an open heart to men anyway. In seven years of teaching these workshops, there has not been one workshop where there was concern expressed about homophobic issues. I have many special memories of helping men feel safe enough to open their hearts to connect through their hearts with another man. You can see the shock and then amazement when they realize how rich this experience is and that it is safe, appropriate, and free of hidden agendas. Once men realize how rich it is to connect with other men through their hearts, they immediately want to share it with their sons, father, and brothers.

In a world of love, men would be as free to open their hearts as women. Unfortunately, an open heart does not support fighting wars. Men have carried the burden of this painful task and have learned to collectively close their hearts. Until they have the courage and desire to return to their natural state of love, they frequently have their hearts defended and unavailable to themselves and others. This limits their creative abilities, hurts them, and makes them vulnerable to stress-related diseases. The ones who empower and awaken their hearts open their lives to new levels of warmth, creative abilities, and love. Their lives become warmer, healthier, and easier once the barricades are broken down.

When individuals connect with men who have studied opening their hearts, they are amazed at their warmth, presence, and masculinity. They inspire any who meet them. They love to grow together and support each other in creating their dreams. The purity of their hearts is important to them, and they set a powerful example for other men fearful of opening their hearts.

For women: Do you feel that men have an equally powerful ability to live true to an open, loving heart? . . . Are you afraid of men who have open and loving hearts? . . . Do you desire to put down or disrespect men with open hearts?

For men: Are you open to supporting living what you love? . . . What are your fears about opening your heart in your daily life? . . . Do you demand an intimate relationship to provide the possibility for opening your heart, or are you capable of living with an open heart without an intimate relationship?

Pearl Thirty

Laughing, Laughing, Laughing

Years ago, when I was first awakening my emotional body, I heard that laughter was very beneficial and healthy. I decided that I would devote an hour a day to laughing as deeply as I could. The first three expressive laughs usually were difficult. After that, the absurdness of my laughter became funny to me. Then the laughter had its own momentum, and I went along for the joyous ride.

I had a friend who lived in Alaska whom I called one night. The minute I heard her voice, the laughing began spontaneously, uninvited. I spent almost an hour on the phone with her and could say nothing. All I could do was laugh. Naturally, she laughed, too. For us this was totally fun, spontaneous, and brought a rich experience into our lives. I love when something suddenly kicks on inside, and we unshackle our restrictions and allow our hearts to stream through us with all of God's love in the form of laughter. It feels so alive.

At a recent seminar, I was sharing with my students sitting around the table about my laughing an hour a day for about a year as deeply as I could. Soon they were insisting that I unshackle myself in front of them and laugh in a way that I had not done in six or seven years. Once I began, other students came to the table and surrounded it to share in the fun. The laughter was contagious and recharged everyone who was tired from the personal growth work of the workshop. I had a great time sharing and teaching the brave ones who learned how to laugh this way.

Laughter is always available to us. We can get so focused on trying to grow and evolve that we forget that this magical gift from God is available whether something is funny or not. It always moves us forward out of fear.

Sometimes I feel that I laugh because I am so scared. When it occurs, I recognize this particular laughter immediately and quickly deal with the fear behind it. I know the reason that I created this laughter was that I understood the power of laughter. At my most terrified moments, I create laughter to protect myself from emotional terror. I instinctively understand that if I laugh, then God's love makes it all the way into my body. This is my greatest protection. The laughter prevents me from going into shock, which shuts off a powerful connection to God and makes me vulnerable to whatever I am afraid of.

Are you willing to use laughter to enrich your life? . . . . There is no emotional pain that can sustain itself in the presence of deep laughter. The laughter simply allows the body to expel the negative emotions out through the movement. As these toxic feelings leave, we get the additional benefit of feeling the joy of laughter.

See how many expressive and unusual laughs you can make. Laughter tapes are a great way to start. Laughter truly frees your heart to allow your life to be more dynamic, loving, and alive.

Pearl Thirty-One

Humor and My Heart

For most of my life, I was too shy to participate in any kind of theatrical performance because it terrified me. About fifteen years ago, my creativity exploded open. As part of that experience, I was invited to put on a costume and create a video with friends. Instead of panicking and refusing, which would have been my normal pattern, I surprised myself by fully birthing the deeply repressed comedienne inside.

Once I released my comedienne, one of my favorite forms of play was to create an opportunity to let her loose. She seemed to be unlimited in her creative expression. All I had to do was to bring her forward, and out would come an extemporaneous skit which was as new to me as it was to my students and friends.

Laughter is one of the most powerful ways to deal with trapped, painful emotions. So during intensives when people were tired, I let my comedienne entertain the students. I would have a wonderful time, and our students would laugh and release trapped emotions. Everyone would get re-energized for further transformational work.

One day the students were too tired to continue without rest. I eagerly decided to do a skit. The students gathered around me waiting for the fun, as I stood up to do one of my favorite things. Usually, within a second or two, the creative stream would flow and off I would go to my own delight as well as the delight of my audience.

This time was different; I felt, I listened, I trusted, and I could sense nothing. It felt as though I no longer had the key to access that part of me. My comedienne was nowhere to be found, and I was uncertain what to do. After an uncomfortable period, I realized that I could no longer allow the comedienne inside to use patterns offensive to a purified heart.

As my students sighed with disappointment as I explained this, I sat down to explore humor in harmony with a purified heart. I realized humor that belittled me or anyone else had, over the past months, become increasingly uncomfortable.

Critical humor was an easy place for me to go. I knew that my storytelling ability and comedienne came from my father and his mother. Both of them were funny and loved to tell stories as much as I do. As I reviewed the humor of our lineage, I realized it was always making fun of someone, and that someone was usually me. I could no longer use this because it hurt and offended my heart.

I remember the pain of my father's humor as a child. He would make fun of me as an expression of his humor. Its effect was debilitating. I created other men in my life that did the same thing. It never occurred to me to tell them how much this hurt me. Instead, I would pretend it was okay or funny. I'm sure they believed I liked it. As I reviewed my comedienne's humor, I realized how easy it was for her to make me the brunt of the joke or make fun of someone else. I obviously had been assigned the task to clean up this part of my humor, so I no longer offended my purified heart or the purified hearts of others.

I used to create a humorous situation by twisting the situation around. The story appeared to go one direction, and out of nowhere, I suddenly took the audience in an unexpected direction. As I explored this, I realized that this was another area to address.

Because of the power and authority that my teachings carried in terms of assisting individuals in restructuring their hearts, my words were deeply felt and valued. People listened carefully to what I said—even words of jest. I realized that in my stories and humor it was important that I not twist situations or tell untruths that might be confusing or unclear to others. Although it was done to cause people to laugh, that twisting around of the situations might leave a residue in people's minds that worked against their highest good. Because they trusted and respected my teachings, my heart was very uncomfortable with this.

So I decided that in order for my comedienne to reappear, she must meet the following criteria: make fun of no one, including myself; always speak truth; and eliminate twisting the situation around to confuse people. It took me over two years to feel that I could meet these criteria to honor and harmonize with a purified heart.

During the talent show for my millennium workshop, my comedienne made a surprise visit. She met all my criteria for a purified heart. My audience was delighted, and I had a wonderful time allowing that part of me to express itself once more. It gave me great joy to give them a memorable punch line that offered the opportunity to bring abundance to them.

Do you create humor that has you bearing the brunt of it? . . ❀ . . Are you ready to heal this part of you that allows others or yourself to hurt and disrespect you through humor? . . ❀ . . Do you go numb or lash out when this occurs, rather than communicating your discomfort from your heart? . ❀ . . Are you open to learning to protect your heart by using phases such as the following?:

"Your humor was not funny to me because it made fun of me and that hurts my heart."

"That hurts. I don't want to be the brunt of your joke." Sometimes people will cover their hurtful comment with, "That was a joke. Can't you take a joke? Don't you have a sense of humor?" Again, it is important for you to be loyal to your heart, as the following phrase relates:

"Any time I am the brunt of a joke, it is not funny to me. I would have to pretend if I displayed anything other than feeling hurt and uncomfortable."

If you draw people into your life who make fun of you, you may want to repeat the above quotes out loud, until you feel comfortable using such phrases to help stop this.

If you do not choose to speak to the person making the critical comments, then feel why you created the unkind treatment. I let both my mind and heart know that bearing the brunt of a joke creates pain for me. By healing my own internal criticism, I heal my tendency to manifest this in my external world.

Explore your humor. Is it mean and belittling with disguised jabs hidden behind the words? . . ❀ . . Is it crude and offensive? . . ❀ . . Or is your humor safe to fully express the beauty and joy of the purity of your heart?

I feel loving-heart humor is the best! It makes our world safe to keep our hearts delightfully open.

Pearl Thirty-Two

Moving Beyond Words

Not everyone is extremely sensitive. This pearl is for the ones who are and struggle with how to integrate their sensitivity in their daily lives in a way that works and blesses them.

Unless you have allowed your heart to experience the vastness of love, words about love are only that—words. My expertise as a heart teacher helps individuals move beyond words to experience awareness inside themselves that connects to the vastness of love. This vastness of love is your birthright whether you choose to claim it or you choose to deny it. It is only here that you can experience the richness that makes life worth living.

Words are created in a rather narrow band of frequencies in our minds. I am using them now to communicate with you. Unless my words assist you in reaching into that vastness of love, feeling, and connection within, these words have little effect in helping you create what you love in your daily life.

Refusing to truly listen on a feeling level to these words is like refusing to acknowledge any other color than purple. Purple allows you to function in this world, but it leaves you with only the mundane rather than the sublime experiences of all other colors.

Our society tends to operate on a rather narrow band of frequencies in our minds, called the mental self. Our mental palette includes words, logic, and analysis often driven by hype. The passionate, intuitive, and sweetly intimate emotions tend to be devalued, ignored, and lost by unrelenting analysis, logic, and criticism. In this mental barrage, we can lose awareness of our feeling heart nature that is part of our birthright.

Our arrogant minds are certain they are all that is valuable and worthwhile, and they lead us away from the emotional and connected experiences that take us into the heart.

If you are not able to feel and access the vastness of love available through your heart, then review the memories of your childhood. Children effortlessly experience an open heart either until they are taught to avoid it or until they receive such physical, emotional, or mental blows to their sensitivity that they withdraw and shut down this part of themselves. If you have shut down this part, then with courage you can open it back up and restore your feeling heart. Tremendous heart treasures await you.

As an adult we can learn how to protect ourselves from vulnerabilities that we were not able to protect ourselves from as children. Our greatest protection is to understand that we create all of our experiences in life, and we are never a victim of them regardless of how painful they may be. In all cases, we are seeking to study and learn. We can graduate out of these painful lessons through learning self-mastery.

As a child, I was extremely sensitive and intuitively aware in a world that had little understanding of how to help me deal with this sensitivity. My dad was also sensitive and intuitive. However, he was probably taught that it was wrong, inappropriate, and unsafe. When he felt I was sensitive, rather than supporting or nurturing me, he would often shock me out of the sensitivity with the message that I was inappropriate, spacey, or something to be made fun of.

Each of you have your own experiences of how your sensitivity was devalued and how you were taught to avoid it. Until you give value back to your true sensing ability, chances are you are still treating yourself the way you were taught as a child.

I now love and value my sensitivity. Truly it is a very beautiful part of who I am. I love assisting others in safely accessing the deep, intense, and sensitive part of themselves. With this sensitivity and awareness restored, individuals become richer in their self-identity. To regain this access in a way that feels good, we must relearn that we can handle this intuitive and sensitive self. The experiences that caused us to feel that we could not handle our sensitive self were based on the false perception that we were victims. As we felt victimized, we disconnected from God, leaving ourselves needy, disconnected, and debilitated.

If your feeling nature is damaged or shut down, then you can learn to open that part of yourself back up. To have the courage to do this, you must know that there is a huge payoff for it. My experience is that restoring the feeling self allows a profound connection into the awareness of your heart and greatly blesses you. Don't run away from a powerful and beautiful part of who you are because of fear and panic. True fulfillment is limited without this sensitive part available, integrated, and comfortable.

Do you keep your reality locked into a mental world where words have all the power and your feeling, intuitive self is denied or devalued? . . ❦ . . Do you fear your sensitivity? . . ❦ . . Are you aware of your true feeling nature? . . ❦ . . Or is that a concept that means nothing to you on a tangible, experiential level? . . ❦ . . Do you desire to reopen this feeling part of yourself?

Learning to open back up and use your sensing abilities brings a richness to your life that is valuable and beautiful. This opens inner doorways—which may be closed due to fear of vulnerability and sensitivity—in order to allow more of your soul into your body and daily life. Once you do, then you can feel the deep feelings behind words. Your heart is waiting to experience the sweetness and richness of awareness of this amazing part of your being.

Chapter Thirty-Three

Listening With My Heart

As I teach, I explain to my students that the real teachings are not in my words, but through the magnitude of God's love that is associated with my words. As part of my teaching skills, I sense when my students are open and receiving this love in their bodies or when they are fearfully blocking it out.

Adjusting the learning experience to help the class stay open to receiving the love behind the words has been an important part of my role as a teacher. This is a difficult concept to understand, because our physical world tends to be so focused on the words themselves.

Each time I taught my fusion science class, I would reiterate the importance of this. I would prepare them by saying, "Those of you who try to get this information with your mind will only get a tiny piece. It is bigger than your mental self can understand. It is through your feeling self that you experience the depth in your body of what I am truly teaching you." Frequently, the less technical or less mentally focused students, who were more accustomed to experiencing life with their feeling self rather than their minds, had the most profound experience of the fusion science class.

In this class, a woman who is a deeply feeling person started asking questions. Soon she turned beet-red and laughed for the remaining two hours of the class. When I realized that she couldn't contain the magnitude of what she was feeling, I simply kept teaching as she continued to experience the feeling of the fusion science in her body through delightful laughter.

The next day she said to me, "Tanai, that was one of the most meaning-ful experiences I have ever had. So much so that I want to draw an atom on my self-love mirror. I feel so connected to the science of fusion." My heart rejoiced. I had no doubt that she had experienced my fusion science class in a tangible and very real way. She had lived the dynamic feeling of the fusion I was teaching rather than collecting facts about the possibility. By allowing herself this experience, she increased her ability to feel the power, joy, and delight of the fusion that can occur within an open heart.

One day as I was teaching, a teenager in my class raised his hand. I could see in his face that something had deeply moved him. He shared, "I got it! When I listen with my heart, I can receive the whole thing. It's bigger than a word or even a book or many books. When I listen with my heart, I feel what is greater than can be understood by words. Your words actually carry the wisdom of many books. I can feel it. When I listen with my heart, I can feel the whole thing."

I smiled wide because I knew he had truly understood through a tangible body experience what I had been sharing with my students for years. I had him stand in front of the class and teach the others how to listen with their hearts.

If you only value constructs of intellect, then you limit how much wis-dom you receive. And if this is your normal pattern, then it also indicates that you limit how much life you allow yourself to feel and experience on a physi-cal level. If, however, you value your heart, then you open up to the true magnitude of teachings which come through the heart. Once you get this understanding, it opens the doorway for your heart to create a more wonder-ful life for yourself based on living what you love—and it feels good, too!

Do you know how to listen with your heart? . . 🌹 . . Are you willing to allow your heart to open enough to permit this? . . 🌹 . . Do you feel safe setting aside your logical, analytical, questioning self which causes your mind to dominate? . . 🌹 . . Do you truly allow yourself to feel if knowledge is true or right for you in your heart without logical interference?

Explore feeling words with your heart with someone you trust. Feel how much more connection and awareness comes once you listen with your heart. It is a rich, beautiful, and blessed way to listen and experience a fuller life.

God's Innernet

Pearl Thirty-Four

Knowing, When I'm Sure I Don't

Not knowing when you need to know is frustrating. The confusion is similar to being in a room of mirrors and not knowing which image is real. After you're through feeling confused, racing in a circle, and distrusting your inner knowing while trying to force an answer, it is a relief to shut down and give up.

Did it ever occur to you that you are the one who chooses to reduce your ability to know? Yes, that's right. You choose to shut down this ability. The good news is that since you are the one who shuts it down, you are also the one who can reawaken your ability to know.

Imagine going around faster and faster in a chaotic race car. Once you start your hectic racing, it would be very difficult to slow down until you decide to. You could race around faster and faster for a very long time until you decide that this doesn't work for you. The racing has in it crazy confusion and scattered patterns that cause you to distrust your knowing. It can also be painfully addictive.

The key is to recognize immediately when you step into your race car. The second that you detect that you are in these patterns, you can choose to pull to the side and get out, much as you chose to race in the first place. You have a few moments to tell your inner mind attendant that you have changed your mind and want out before you are off and racing. If you miss those first few moments before the race car builds momentum, it's harder.

Here's a way to get out when you feel like you are crazy because you don't know. Ask yourself, "What am I feeling?" If you can slow down enough to feel, because feelings are always slower than thoughts, then your mind can get out of your race car and allow your slower feelings to catch up with your fast-paced mind.

Chances are you got in the race car in the first place to escape to your mind because you were upset and afraid. What you don't realize is that when you escape to your mind, these mixed-up feelings upset your heart and your feeling self even more. The fast-paced thoughts literally generate more and more feelings, which then create a huge buildup of emotions unless you slow down to give them time to integrate.

Slowing down and feeling everything allows the crazy electricity to relax in your mind, reduces the momentum of emotions, and allows your feelings to guide you. That way your mind doesn't short circuit or hurt you, and your mind has the time it needs to work out the solution that is best for you. Within a short time, perhaps a night's sleep, the answer comes to you clearly—often in a flash.

When I used to experience the craziness of my mental race car, I did not trust my ability to figure out or know the best answer when this was occurring. The answer was created from chaos and anxiety. Only once I slow down and settle into my feelings, do I know that a wonderful answer can come to me from the quietness of my heart and mind. This answer is based on peace, serenity, and goodness, rather than anxiety and fear.

The next time you create chaos and fear because you don't know, follow these simple steps:

1. Slow down.
2. Ask, "Sweetie, what are you feeling?"
3. Stop trying to figure out an answer.
4. Trust that an answer will come when you relax, let go of your fear, and allow yourself to feel.

When you learn to do this, your tendency to create chaos within you diminishes. Also, you find that your ability to know returns, and you begin to trust that it is always there to support you.

Give yourself time by creating peace inside first, and then you will be surprised to know what you know!

Pearl Thirty-Five

God's Innernet

We have gained unprecedented access to facts and ease of communication through the Internet. For each of us to have the ability to communicate so easily and inexpensively almost anyplace in the world changes the destiny of our planet.

However, I have a secret for you. Our current Internet is preparing us for a much greater Innernet. This Innernet connects us to the unseen worlds which some call God or heaven. God's Innernet provides the opportunity for us to connect to anyone or any information.

While relaxing with two friends one day, our conversation turned to the Internet, and I said, "Our minds have the ability to access wisdom, knowledge, and communication through our ability to merge and connect with God. Our Internet is a first step for humanity to learn this. The Internet is simply a tangible expression of a much greater Innernet of God."

One of my friends, who is an Internet expert, turned pale and immediately became fearful. He physically moved his chair away from me and was obviously very uncomfortable. Seeing how stressful this comment was on him, my other friend and I changed the subject to something less threatening. I was surprised at how much fear this comment evoked because I thought he would be fascinated about where I perceived our Internet to be headed since he is both a successful Internet expert and a student of spiritual studies.

Once he got his balance back, he related, "I am already experiencing that. I communicate through the Internet with people all over the world. Sometimes I dream that I e-mail them, but I don't actually. Then I get an e-mail back the next day, responding to what I didn't write. Other times, I dream about several e-mail exchanges. Later, I learn that all the information exchanged in and learned from my dream is real and applicable. I am already doing exactly what you said. I am communicating through God's Innernet without actually using the Internet."

My other friend and I smiled when he released his fear as he said this. We discussed how our Internet is a tool for humanity to learn a greater level of communication by using God's Innernet. All of us have the ability to receive wisdom and knowledge through our connection to God. We are all comprised of electromagnetic energy down to the atoms that create our physical body. I believe that this electromagnetic energy holds much information, and this awareness is accessible much like the information that is transferred by electromagnetic waves associated with our cell phones.

I am more comfortable and experienced with the Innernet than some people are, yet we all have this ability and use it even if we deny that we do. That is where hunches and flashes of insight come from as well as an innate sense of who you can trust and who you had better avoid.

If I listen to my gut feelings and knowledge that come through my connection to God, my life tends to work well. If I don't, I regret that I ignored my hunches. After enough times of regretting, I learned to listen to God more carefully. For some of us, this is scary, so we tend to block it off. Although, without realizing it, every time we have a hunch or a gut feeling, we are allowing God to provide useful information for us.

Have you blocked God from giving you useful information through your hunches to help your life work better? . . ❧ . . Or are you grateful that God supports you by giving you intuitive guidance and knowledge? . . ❧ . . Does it scare you when you know something before it occurs, or do you feel blessed that God has provided an inside tip for you? . . ❧ . . Have you noticed that when you listen to your intuition that your life moves forward, and when you don't, it stops or jams your creative process? . . ❧ . . Are you willing to explore opening your God-Innernet up to allow intuitive knowledge to guide you in your life?

I love God, and I love that God provides information that helps my life be more peaceful, loving, and successful. God's loving information helps me to feel connected and part of God's creation. This gift is available for anyone who chooses it.

Pearl Thirty-Six

Linking Facts to Love

L et's imagine two gifted students at the best university in the world who agree to an experiment associated with availability of knowledge. The department heads of this outstanding university agree to connect the two students to the best minds and research throughout the world, available on request at all times. Before the students meet each of the department heads, we explain that their hearts are the keys to this experiment.

One of the students gets it immediately and quickly establishes loving bonds with all the department heads. He gets acquainted with their kids, knows their favorite sports, and genuinely loves connecting and making friends with each one of them. When he needs facts or concepts, he would phone to ask, "Joe, how are you? How's the kids? I'm doing research and need some information." Within an instant he would have all the facts or information he needed. His relationships with the department heads are meaningful and a warm part of his life. The student's heart keeps him connected to all the information that is necessary to support connection, love, and life.

Conversely, the other student worships the information. The moment he discovers that the department heads have unlimited access to the best knowledge throughout the world, he wants his mind to know all of it. He gets frustrated that even though he is constantly learning, there is so much more to learn. Being driven to learn more and more, he requests more and more facts which the department heads agree to give him. He hardly knows the department heads. He is much too busy using them to access knowledge to care about them or their lives. In truth, his life is consumed by facts. One day he realizes that his facts mean nothing. His heart is burdened, empty, and lonely. He discovers that he has used the facts to separate himself from his heart and life.

I learned that knowledge only has value to me if it creates more love, sweetness, and richness in my life. Otherwise, knowledge can create stress and pain, something my heart loves to eliminate. For many years of my life, I was hungry for knowledge; I used to say that I wanted to know everything. Today, that is funny to me because now that my spiritual gifts provide so much access to knowledge, I simply desire the knowledge that I need moment by moment. This frees up my awareness to be more available for life, love, and the present moment.

Do you worship knowledge or do you use knowledge to create sweetness and a warm supportive life? . . ❧ . . Do you link knowledge with love? . . ❧ . . If so, how? . . ❧ . . Does this influence the richness of your life? . . ❧ . . Are you willing to settle for a life that is focused on obtaining facts at the cost of your heart? . . ❧ . . Or like the first student, are you choosing to create a wealth of love that supports you having all the facts you need available to you when you need them?

It is a choice. When you choose knowledge that supports love, you will be amazed at how fulfilling this knowledge is.

Feelings, Feelings, Feelings

Pearl Thirty-Seven

Thoughts and Feelings

Your thoughts are fast . . .

Your feelings are slow . . .

A lot of thoughts create a lot of feelings . . .

Experiencing too many feelings without giving them time to move through your body creates lack of awareness and a knot of feelings . . .

Lack of awareness of feelings creates numbness, which leaves you out of touch with love, passion, and creativity . . .

Knotted-up feelings create stress, pain, and even disease . . .

Awareness of feelings creates a life that is worth living . . .

To experience a life that is worth living, slow down and learn to feel . . .

If you have too many knotted feelings inside, then
you may perceive all feelings are negative and painful . . .

But feelings can be positive: joy, ecstasy, and connection . . .

Are you willing to untangle your feelings and
slow down to experience the pleasure of life? . . .

How alive do you desire to feel? . . .

Breathe . . . Slow down . . . Feel . . .

Feelings are slow . . .

Love your feelings and allow them to bless your world. This will make all the difference in the quality of your life.

Pearl Thirty-Eight

How to Unload My Overload

When I am overwhelmed, I can walk past a leaf in my home for days, each time desiring the leaf to be removed, yet perceiving that I can't bend down and pick it up. I can look at clothes tossed on the floor, and every cell in my body tells me I have no ability to put the clothing in their appropriate place. It's a feeling that tells me I have no ability to express what I love on the physical level. The best I can hope for is surviving with the minimum physical expression necessary.

What happens to throw us into this numbing state is that our emotional bodies get overloaded. It is a cry for help, "Slow down . . . stop the demands . . . let me catch up." When we have a lot of thoughts, especially when we are rapidly changing or under undo stress, our mental selves push us faster than what our slower emotional bodies can keep up with.

Our mental wheels simply spin faster than our slower emotional wheels. Something has to give or the wheels get more and more out of synchronization with each other. As this occurs, an individual has basically two options. One option which supports peaceful resynchronization is to slow down or rest the mental self to give the emotional self time to catch up. Backing off the mental demands to give the emotional self time to catch up is a very loving thing to do during emotional overload. People who are aware of and value their hearts will consistently choose this.

The other option we may choose when we are overwhelmed can and does tend to create long-lasting damage. This option is to shut down or numb our feeling self so that all we are aware of is our thoughts. In an overloaded state, these thoughts tend to race faster, push harder, and create chaos, body pain, and stress. This choice tends to be standard operating procedure for the typical stressed American. Once the choice is made, one's emotional body stops functioning and becomes damaged and backed up with toxic negative feelings. If an individual does not give him or herself emotional time to clear the backup, disease is often the result.

While teaching extremely powerful intensives, I often felt overwhelmed with regard to my home. Dirty dishes, dirty clothes dropped wherever I happen to be when I removed them, stacks of unopened mail, and leaves tracked in would pile up so that after five days, my home would look like a mini disaster. For years, I accepted this consequence of teaching, feeling that the demands of this kind of work was creating the problem.

However, one day I couldn't handle one more walk past the leaf. I wanted to be really compassionate with myself because I understood how huge the energy requirements were on me during the intensives. At the same time, I knew that the leaf on my floor was not bringing me joy. So I sat down by the leaf and held my arms around myself and let myself know that I was there one hundred percent for me. I set by the leaf and felt until I could actually feel what was overloading my emotional body. Very compassionately, I was there for myself. The emotions moved, and as I stood up, I picked up the leaf and placed it in the trash.

Afterward, I sat down next to the pile of dirty clothes. Again, I held my arms around myself in a loving way until the blocked emotions cleared and my heart knew how much I cared for and loved myself. As I got up, the pile of dirty clothes came with me. I smiled as I placed them in the clothes basket. It was amazingly easy.

Then I went to the dirty dishes piled up in my sink and again held myself, feeling the "piled up" emotions. As I did, my heart opened, and the dirty dishes made it effortlessly into the dishwasher.

Since I did this, things don't seem to pile up anymore, even when I am under the stress of a seminar that requires much from me. If they do, again I would be there for myself, not to demand anything, but to let myself know that even when I give huge energies to others, I still am very present to support my own needs.

What causes you to feel overloaded? . . . . Are you patiently there for yourself, or are you demanding and critical? . . ✿ . . Are you willing to slow down and really be present for yourself? . . ✿ . . Are you willing to let yourself know how much you care about yourself when you feel over-loaded? . . ✿ . . Are you willing to be very supportive of your needs, whatever they may be?

Giving time for your emotional needs allows you to free yourself of overload. As you do, what you desire to experience and create in your physical life can then manifest as your heart's desire.

Pearl Thirty-Nine

Taking My Life Back From Out-of-Control Rage

Some people have a very short fuse before they explode into violent or potentially violent rage. If you are one of these people, you've got about three to eight seconds from the moment you know you are upset to prevent a potentially horrible or destructive action on your part.

Here's what you can do while you are in a peaceful place. Remember how it feels when your rage begins. Do you want to punch, hurl violent words, or break something? Notice the hugeness of the energy as the rage explodes. In order to diffuse it, you must plan ahead. With only three to eight seconds, there simply isn't any time to figure out a loving approach then. You must decide what you are going to do with the explosive energy before you hit critical mass.

For example, consider a person desiring to hurl his fist or attack anything or anyone once the fuse is lit. In order for his fist or hands not to receive the destructive force, that energy must go somewhere that won't hurt. An appropriate plan of action would be to push, with all his might, all of the negative energy through his feet, pushing, pushing, pushing into the ground until the desire to hurl his fist or attack no longer exists.

Practicing how to handle the rage before you feel it is very important. This is not a cure-all—for this type of rage is evidence of deep, deep hurt which needs to be addressed by trained professionals. However, this technique may help you to prevent hurting yourself or someone else in the meantime.

If you are someone who hurls destructive words at others and would like to stop, try this. Before your fuse goes off, cough, laugh, or sneeze three times as dramatically as possible. Any of these physical releases moves large charges of emotional energy. If they don't clear the negative emotional charge, then say, "Let's talk later." Once you have had time to feel what hurt you and deal with your emotions, then go back to the individual and discuss what you feel.

Rage is always evidence of deep hurt within you where you have denied love. Ultimately, learning how to love yourself and give yourself love is how to eliminate these destructive patterns. As you learn to master your tendency to react violently, you will learn to give yourself the greatest possible love at the moment you feel the rage.

Is rage a frightening part of your life? . . ❦. . If so, do you feel justified in keeping it, or are you ready to heal and release this self-destructive pattern? . . ❦. . Are you willing to face the pain that created your rage?

Remember, *the meaner the rage, the bigger the hurt that caused it, and the greater the love necessary to heal it.*

Pearl Forty

Jealousy

J ealousy is such a miserable feeling. It makes our stomachs knot up and causes us to do things that are very unloving. Years ago, when I first began my spiritual journey, I struggled with jealousy daily. I created as my best friend a lady who was very gifted with spiritual abilities. Her spiritual gifts were as easy for her as breathing, but they made me feel inferior, and I struggled daily to heal that part of me. After a while, I knew I was toxic with jealousy toward my friend. At that time in my life, all I knew to do with negative emotions was attempt to hang on and trust that God would help me through the pain.

As I drove to work one day during this time, I saw a port-a-potty burning on the side of the road. I pulled to the median nearby and in a panic evaluated my options on what to do about the burning port-a-potty. What do you do with a burning port-a-potty? I didn't have a clue. I thought about using my little vehicle fire extinguisher, but somehow risking my life and extinguisher for this cause left me cold and uncertain.

I thought about driving to the nearby fire station with all the emotions that were churning inside me to desperately plead, "Please, come quickly! Come save the burning port-a-potty!" Even with my natural flair for the dramatic, I instinctively knew this would be a difficult one to live down.

I thought about going to work and calling the fire department. My pain was so huge, I finally decided that I would pull back into the traffic so I wouldn't be late to work, which would have created a new set of problems.

Later that day, I shared with my friend my anxiety about the burning port-a-potty. Not until I shared this with her did I see any humor in this situation. In fact, if anything, I felt guilty that I had not saved the port-a-potty. She laughed for twenty minutes until finally the humor of the situation penetrated through my pain. Then I laughed too. I could see that my burning port-a-potty was a wonderful symbol of what was happening inside me as my jealousy was being burned up and transmuted.

That evening I decided I would return to the site of the burning port-a-potty to see its fate and make peace with the guilt that I had not saved it. I drove back to the construction site. There was no evidence that it ever existed. There was not one ash or a single indentation in the sand to say anything had ever been there. I released this one to the great mystery.

I help my students walk through jealousy so much more easily and faster than I could when I began pursuing my spiritual path. If one understands what causes jealousy, it is easier to heal. Jealousy is the emotion that comes from blocking or denying a part of you that is valuable and that your heart desires to awaken. People are only jealous if they deny something they love and value about themselves.

Jealousy is not generated with a special gift you have no interest in or have already integrated into your life. In others words, I would not have been jealous of a great football player who appeared to have it all, because I do not desire to be a football player. However, I was jealous of my friend's spiritual gift because that was where my soul was crying for me to open up.

My friend had not denied her spiritual abilities. I had. My heart knew that my spiritual abilities had to be opened back up for me to share the teachings I was meant to. I panicked because I blocked and limited those abilities at that time in my life. She was my wake-up call saying, "Tanai, open back up. Your spiritual gifts are important and necessary for your service."

I tell my students to focus as little as possible on the person providing their wake-up call. Other than identifying what the other person is showing about themselves that they have blocked, the rest is really not important. In other words, being jealous of my friend really only had significance in showing me how much of my spiritual ability I had chosen to block. If she had not been there to show this to me, I would have no doubt created someone else to play that role for me. Getting upset with her was a waste, because she was providing a valuable service for me.

When you learn to focus on the message rather than the messenger, the jealousy is less threatening. You see clearly what parts of yourself you must unlock for your heart to express the fullness of your potential. Try feeling what the person who you are jealous of has allowed themselves to develop that you have refused to allow. Then put focus on opening those hidden gifts inside yourself. It is so much more pleasurable than staying locked up and continuing to feel those miserable jealous feelings that you have created as a wake-up call to let you know that similar abilities and gifts rest inside you.

Who are you jealous of? . . . . . What traits do they have that generate feelings of jealousy inside you? . . . . . Do you negatively respond to these people, perhaps seeking to hurt or diminish them? Or do you focus on loving and developing for yourself what you admire and are jealous of in them?

Jealousy can be used to hurt you or as a signpost of where valuable and useful parts of you are locked up. What you are jealous of shows the traits your heart wants to reclaim within you in order to experience something you love.

Pearl Forty-One

Getting a Grip on My Feelings

A long time ago, I was focused on learning how to feel my own feelings and how to allow others to see and feel them. I had learned to guard my feelings by showing no one what I truly felt. I experienced the fear of dying if I came close to being emotionally expressive or honest with others about my feelings. It was a miserable prison to be in, because my true nature is rich with glorious feelings. However, at this time in my life, those amazing feelings were locked behind a stoic mask.

I traveled from Asheville, NC to Florida for a healing session for the express purpose of opening my emotional body. Mostly we focused on father issues. As I got in my car for the ten-hour drive back to North Carolina, I was convinced that I had completed my father issues. I soon found that this was not the case.

Once I returned, I felt more emotions than probably I had ever experienced. Whenever the man I was dating didn't do exactly as I wanted, I would burst into a fit of tears and emotional tantrums. Never in my life had I experienced such a wide range of emotions.

I was expressing feelings in a way I had never experienced. I could feel the actress inside of me feeling how far she could use her emotions to push situations. In the midst of tears and drama as she was expressing that life could not go on without this man doing as I pleased, she would periodically peek out to see how well things were going. Obviously, whatever was happening inside me was creating havoc in my relationship.

After about three weeks of this emotional binge, the man I was dating said, "Tanai, I think I'd better back up a bit and let you get a grip on these emotions." This set in motion a whole new wave of drama that included the end of the relationship. With my attempt to deal with father issues, I opened up a can of worms inside myself.

I knew that I had a painful experience with my father when I was four years old that had shut me down. He hurt my feelings so deeply that I had no way to continue life as I knew it after this. One day I was so full of life and enthusiasm that people wanted to be around me for the excitement and energy; the next day I withdrew, stopped speaking, and tended to be quiet and alone. As a result of this trauma, my emotional self stopped maturing through normal stages of development, locked in the patterns of a typical four-year old. Somehow, the session to deal with my father reconnected me to my four-year-old emotional self. Suddenly, I was an emotional child in an adult's body.

As difficult as this was, I am so grateful for the experience. I loved being that emotionally free and expressive. Obviously, the feelings were very immature and inappropriate. However, they were also full of passion and had no fear of letting others see them. As an adult, I got to experience a normal stage of development for a passionate four-year-old child with acting abilities.

Much learning and good came from this. A healer friend helped me move into appropriate age responses. During three weeks of emotional gymnastics and theatrics, I pulled down some of the rigid barriers that prevented me from letting others know or see that I had feelings. And, I later discovered that I had only opened the doorway to see my father issues rather than completing them.

I am so grateful that I am no longer trapped in that isolating cage. I am also grateful that I emotionally matured and am capable of creating what I love. I deeply appreciate life experiences such as this that have helped awaken my feeling self and matured it into a part of me that is valuable and beautiful.

Are you emotionally alive and honest? . . . . . Is your emotional self mature, stable, and supportive of passion and creativity? . . . . . Or is it trapped in immature patterns of a child or teenager? . . . . . Are you willing to heal, so that you can have an expressive and loving emotional nature?

If you have given up your emotional self to pretend and remain locked into a non-feeling world, you have an amazing option. The ability to reclaim your emotional self is within you. For those who desire life to be real and alive, it is a journey not to be missed.

Pearl Forty-Two

My Thoughts and Emotions Create My Reality

If you are unaware that your thoughts and emotions create your reality, then life happens to you. Let's say that you are irritated about not getting the attention you feel you deserve from your husband. You want him to create something special for your anniversary tomorrow, and it is obvious he doesn't remember.

Upset, you walk through your home. Suddenly your upset mind focuses on something you don't like about your home. Perhaps you desire a new carpet but have not yet created it. Soon your irritation with your husband turns into hatred for the aging carpet.

A few hours later, your child spills a full glass of grape juice on the carpet you have been hating for hours. You scream at your child, and threaten punishment, blaming him or her for the damage to the carpet. Unless you are aware of your emotions and how that which is inside you manifests outside, you are certain that the ugly grape juice spill was your child's fault.

When your husband comes home, you scream at him telling him his kid damaged the ugly carpet, and you are fed up with both him and your child! Ouch! This is a common hangout ground for people until they learn that their thoughts and feelings create their reality.

Let's replay the above scene with the awareness that our thoughts and emotions are creating our reality. Your husband does not mention your anniversary. You can feel that this means a lot to you and that you must adjust the situation within yourself quickly to greater self-love to receive the attention and love you desire.

You can feel you are upset. You walk through your house. You sense that you want to attack the aging carpet because of disappointment with your husband. You say to yourself, "Sweetie, I know you are upset with him. We can turn this around if we love ourselves enough. Hating my home will only make it worse. I know this carpet is old, but let's love it a moment to help it last a bit longer." You pause and focus on loving the carpet.

You can feel your body bristle when your child comes near you. Again you speak to yourself, "Sweetie, it's not my child's fault I'm upset. Relax. It's going to be okay." Sensing how upset and unavailable you are, your child begins to make demands. You answer, "Mommie is going to be all right. I'm upset and need some quiet time to let everything feel better inside me. Could you give me about ten minutes of quiet time? When I come back, I can be more present for you." At first your child starts to make further demands, but as you relax so does your child. He or she runs off to play with toys sensing your ability to deal with being upset. This releases your child's fear that you can't handle the situation.

You go to your quiet chair and begin to feel how scared you are that your husband doesn't care or doesn't pay attention the way you desire. As you feel this, the dark cloud starts lifting. You start giving yourself love. You remember some of your special anniversaries. You realize that he has planned some of them, and you have planned others. Then you have a wonderful idea of what you would love to share with him on your anniversary tomorrow. You can feel how much you love him. As you relax, you remember how he attempted to be affectionate with you this morning. You were too upset about the anniversary to let him. You relax and look forward to sharing your idea about celebrating your anniversary with him.

Moment by moment, we make choices to love and hold true to the desire to love, or we choose to stay a victim and deny ourselves love. In one scenario, we create what we love. In the other one, we seldom get what our hearts' desire. We choose to remain a victim who creates only pain.

Can you feel, see, and understand how your thoughts and feelings create the quality of your life? . . . . Are you a victim of them, fated to be painfully jerked around by them without recourse? Or can you clearly feel and see the patterns that hurt you, and then make more self-loving choices? .

.✿... Do you use blame to distract yourself from taking responsibility for creating what you love?

Living a heart-centered life requires moment-by-moment choosing love rather than fear. The victories of this are the best!

Pearl Forty-Three

Taking Responsibility for Me

A close friend and I were having lunch with another lady. The lady shared that she did not feel her mate would live much longer due to an illness, and she was preparing for this transition. She mentioned that she had recently discovered that she unknowingly used her mate as a reason to live. As a result, her mate had to hang onto life to assure that she had a reason to live. Once she realized this, she saw how she had placed this heavy burden on her mate. She released it, freeing her mate of that responsibility. Once she did, everything got better for both of them.

After the lady shared this story, she turned and asked my friend a question. She knew that my friend and I were close, although we were not in an intimate relationship. This was a time in which I was needy and had depended on my friend for extra support. I was especially fragile physically and emotionally. The lady said, "Are you willing to let Tanai go even if it meant that she might not choose to live?"

My friend sat there for a few moments feeling nervous and uncertain. Our friendship meant a lot to both of us, and she was aware that at that time I was deeply dependent on her for emotional strength.

She looked at the lady, knowing that what she spoke was true. I sat there, watching what was happening and feeling as though my destiny was being negotiated in front of my eyes. Eventually, I could see in my friend's face that she was releasing the responsibility that she had taken on to keep me alive.

When she did, my body shook, and I felt as though I had been standing on a tall fence post and suddenly lost my balance. At that instant, I knew that if I chose to die that she would not hold me back or take any responsibility to convince me to do otherwise. It is a very strange feeling when in one moment, you can trust that someone is there to try to make everything all right and support your neediness, and in the next moment she's not.

This was a very important day in my life. I am so grateful that my friend released me. I got to fully accept that if I stayed on Earth, it was because I was creating what I loved. I gave myself permission to let either choosing to live or not live be acceptable. Eventually, I made the decision that I wanted to stay for *me* rather than for my son, my friend, or my work. This decision bumped me into a new creative pattern.

As I took complete responsibility for my joy and life, I could feel that I was the best one to create what I loved. No one else could ever provide the level of support that I desired. I could see that if I was needy and dependent on anyone else for joy or the motivation to live, then I would be robbed of the richness I am capable of living. I loved the transition into investing fully in creating my own rich life rather than depending on anyone to fix it or make it better.

Are you using someone else to motivate you to live? . . ❧. . If so, are you denying your own creative power to create a life that works well for you? . . ❧. . Do you prop up someone or take responsibility for giving her or him a reason to live?

Perhaps if you released this responsibility back, this person would choose to do a more capable job than you could. If you are propping him or her up, chances are that it exhausts you and is perceived as never being enough. From experience, the best result came from me taking responsibility for my life and happiness. Perhaps it is time for you to reclaim that responsibility for yourself. Or maybe it is time for you to release back to anyone the responsibility you have accepted for giving him or her a reason to live. You will be amazed how freed up you feel once you do!

What's Inside Me Pops Outside

Pearl Forty-Four

What My External World Tells Me About My Internal World

If you desire to create what your heart desires, one of the most powerful gifts of information I can share with you is the following. *Your external world is a perfect reflection of your internal world.* This is a truth that is confirmed in many spiritual traditions.

I believe the light of God that creates our bodies is centered within our hearts and within the nuclei of every atom. This light creates an effect similar to a projector in a movie theater. Whatever is going on inside you appears on the screen, as the light of God projects the images of life from within you. The clarity of love within affects how you perceive and create the events and people in your life.

If your heart is clear and pure, then your images, and therefore life, are equally pure. That is why two different people in the same situation can perceive two totally different situations. They have different thoughts, beliefs, and patterns through which the light of God must pass in order to create and perceive life.

The reason this is so exciting and powerful is that you can always know where you are in your creative process. By knowing this, you then sense how to adjust whatever is blocking your creation, similar to having a piece of dirt or a cap in front of the movie projector.

The experience of buying and selling real estate for myself and assisting my students to buy theirs has provided many opportunities to study this. Say you find your dream home. You play the numbers and determine that it is a stretch, but within reach. Your heart is longing for this beautiful expression of you. However, as you get closer to writing the contract or completing the deal, you must stay vigilant to keep yourself from sabotaging what your heart desires.

I was teaching this in a workshop. I described to my students how once you get closer to completion of the deal, you are more likely to get scared. Your fear might cause you to find the most insignificant thing you can to shut your creative process down. I went into much detail about how you might decide you hated the color of the tile in an obscure, seldom-used guest bath and refuse to complete the deal.

After my long discourse with lots of details about this obscure bathroom, I learned that one of the students in the workshop who wanted to buy a home did exactly that. She got scared and decided to hate the color of the tile in the guest bath in order to give in to her fear and not complete the deal. Had she been more aware at that time, she could have realized that she was sabotaging the deal out of fear. She could have uplifted her fear by finding a more realistic way to handle the situation. Obviously, if there had been a structural problem or something of profound significance, she would have known there were different issues inside her. Hers was an insignificant issue associated with color and could have easily been resolved had she dealt with her fear.

Another student was ready to close on her dream home. Unexpectedly, a complex title issue surfaced, one that the lawyers assured her could not be overcome. The deal fell apart. When she shared this with her nine-year-old daughter, her daughter grabbed her mother's self-love mirror. Her daughter volunteered to help her mother do the self-love work to increase their self-love so together they could create the home they desired.

The mother and daughter went to work bumping up their self-love. Within a few months, the title problems that the lawyers were certain could not be corrected were fixed, and the price of the house was reduced by an extra five thousand dollars. The picture she saw in her external world showed her that she did not have enough self-love to allow herself to have a clear title to her dream home. Once she and her daughter increased their self-love, the home was theirs for less than the original cost.

This tool of looking at your external world to know where you are in your internal world is tremendously powerful. If your external world reflects what you love, then you know that your internal world is correctly aligned with patterns of love. If your external world points out problems, then you can see that there is something inside that needs to be restructured to assist you in creating what you love. It takes you from being a victim of your world to being a powerful creator. *Again, by changing something inside you, you can shift your physical reality to support what your heart desires!*

When your physical world does not support what you desire, do you rage and blame the physical world? . . . . Or do you look inside yourself to find what within you did not support your creation?

So often, even if you do not know which pattern inside you prevents you from creating what you love, increasing your self-love supports you moving forward.

Pearl Forty-Five

Creating What Appears to Be Impossible

In order to move forward in my spiritual teachings, I agreed to buy a house. I had lived off of savings for the prior three years and had little confidence I could continue to support myself as my savings dwindled. The thought of any financial commitment was overwhelming. Before my divorce and quitting my job, money was something that was easy for me to create; now it was not.

As I looked for homes I could afford, I would cry. I had been used to beautiful homes, and settling for something less than that caused me pain. I had no income, savings only big enough to buy a lot, and no down payment. Conclusion: I could afford nothing I wanted.

As I drove away from the last house, depressed about the situation, my inner guidance asked me, "What does your heart want?"

Immediately, my heart burst out, "A four thousand square foot home!"

"So be it. Start creating it," my intuition replied.

Even though I had nothing to support the notion that I could create my dream home other than good credit and enough money to purchase a lot, I started dreaming, feeling, and loving what would be my new four thousand square foot home.

After purchasing the property, I went to the contractor to begin the process of building my home. She asked about my finances. When I related them to her, she pointed to a one thousand square foot home. I will never forget what happened. I told her as I pointed to a twenty-four hundred square foot home, "But I want the big one."

She looked at me with a strange look while her body moved back and forth a little bit like someone standing on a vibrating machine as she said, "Oh, okay." She used her calculator to play some kind of numbers game and then told me that I could qualify for the twenty-four hundred square foot home.

I learned a lot from this. I learned not to settle for something if my heart wanted something else. I learned that when I clearly spoke what my heart desired, the doorway would open to help me create what I love. Using this understanding, a few months later I increased the plans from the twenty-four hundred square foot home to the four thousand square foot home my heart passionately desired and, a year later, completed building it.

Do you settle for less than your heart desires? . . . . Are you afraid to speak what you love? . . . . Do you give up and settle for less if you encounter resistance to what you love?

Had I not had the courage to speak up for what I desired, I could be living in a space much smaller than what my heart wanted, disgruntled that God did not give me what I desired. I am glad I didn't stay silent.

Pearl Forty-Six

Keeping My Cool

When I built my dream home, I tackled what appeared to be impossible. Every aspect of it was a stretch. I was scared to death while I was creating this home because I had been so far away from my true creative abilities on the physical level. Several years before, I quit my engineering job to focus on developing the heart technologies that have become part of my teachings. During this time I made little or no money.

When I began working on the loan and commitment to build my home, I had no tangible income, down payment, tax records of income, or any of the other legal documents normally necessary to get a loan to build a home. Getting a loan to build a twenty-four hundred square foot home under these circumstances was truly an accomplishment of taking my love of God and translating this love into creative power. As I committed to build my home, a stream of income materialized out of nowhere to provide a sizeable down payment.

While in this process, I went to my genius Italian loan officer. I told him that the loan for a twenty-four hundred square foot home—that was already a huge stretch for me—was not big enough. I explained that I had found the plans of my dream home, which was four thousand square foot, and I wanted it!

Once I let him know what I desired, he exploded. Papers were tossed around the room like bullets. He yelled at me and mirrored every fear I had.

"You have no business buying an expensive home! Get back into those less expensive plans! You can't handle the payments! I won't give you a penny more than what you are already qualified for now!" He went on storming back and forth for over twenty minutes. I ducked when necessary and listened carefully to everything he said. I knew he was showing me what I was thinking and feeling.

I walked out of his office saying to myself, "Wow! You are one scared cookie." I went home and felt deeply what to do. I had pushed hard to get the original loan. Through his genius, he helped me through the maze of my financial disempowerment and helped me qualify for a loan. I did this on faith because at that time I had no source of income. Once I got my loan, my school began and was very successful, and I had income that could make monthly payments for a larger home.

However, I was emotionally drained from pushing myself into building a home when I was financially impoverished. Now I was stubbornly asking myself to double the ante and create a home that was twice as big. My friend mirrored to me how scared and frazzled I was through his explosion. I couldn't push any longer.

I released my home back to God saying, "God, I know that my dream home does not have this much stress in it. I believe the four thousand square foot home is my home. However, I am tired and cannot push any longer. I am releasing this to you." I did not look at plans or try to create my home in any way during the next three months, other than doing a soothing, powerful manifestation relaxation that I teach in *Creating Your Heart's Desire* workshop. I gave up any desire to push or make anything happen.

My loan officer friend called out of the blue right before Christmas and said, "Get down here! We've got to work on your loan." Calmly, I went to his office. I knew he would tell me where I was in my creative process. I had not lost any desire to create my dream home, I simply knew I could not push anymore to create it. God would have to carry the load; I had already done all I could.

"How much money did you say you needed?" he jabbed. I gave him the amount for the four thousand square foot home, uncertain what would occur when I did. He looked me in the eyes and smiled as he said, "That's not enough. You need money for this, and that, and this, and that." I was unprepared for my friend to play the role of Santa Claus. Soon the rapidly building loan grew past my comfort zone. To allay my fear, I had him reduce the amount by some and left his office knowing that I was going to be successful in manifesting my dream home.

The amount of serenity that I created inside myself through my peace with God worked amazingly well. Through rest and quietness with God, my frazzled mental and emotional selves returned to enough calm to signal to me that what I was creating would be successful. With that message, my friend felt confident that I would be able to make my house payments. He trusted me because I was peaceful and harmonious, which I felt because I had released the creation of my home to God.

Later, as my home came closer to being completed, I had to return to him and ask for even more money. Each time I did, I knew that I needed to be in a state of peace when I did. I got the increased money without an explosion from him because I used peace within me to create what I loved. My inner peace disarmed the caution lights and let him support me rather than kick me out of his office with a verbal tirade.

Notice your response when a person or organization does not give you what you desire. Does this throw you immediately into the blaming patterns of a victim, or do you go inside yourself to find what prevented you from being successful in creating what you love?

If you choose victimization patterns, then you experience hurt from the disappointment and sense of loss. In addition, you decrease your probability of success. However, if you choose heart-based creative patterns, then you create the opportunity to heal the patterns that created the initial problem—and increase your probability of creating what you love.

Don't waste a moment hating, blaming, or resenting people who do not deliver what you feel you desire. When this occurs, something inside you is off and preventing them from supporting you. When you adjust it inside yourself by bringing peace to the frightened, chaotic, and overwhelmed parts of you, your external world shifts. When it does, you not only heal a hurt and frightened part of you, but also have the opportunity to create what you want.

Pearl Forty-Seven

Doing What You Do

There were many times in the creation of my home that it appeared that something would block or stop it. My loan officer, who was extremely intuitive, was always the one to pick this up and let me know that there was or soon would be a problem. He had observed how I worked and knew I had an unusual ability to pull things out of the hole.

Once my friend suggested as he amusingly rolled his eyes, "Whatever you do when you do what you do—you need to do it now." I was an enigma to him; I made him nervous because he did not understand how I made things happen. The mystery was simple. If he told me there was a problem, then I knew the problem was inside me. So when he told me that there were nit-picking issues with the loan that could stop it from coming through, I knew exactly how to handle it. First, I had to get very peaceful and as free of fear as possible. Then I needed to create a stable place inside me that would increase the odds going in my favor. I knew chaos worked against me and might cause the loan company to find an insignificant excuse to stop the loan.

Before a meeting about the loan, I always washed my van to assure as much chaos as possible was removed. In addition, I straightened my desk and cleared away anything that looked like chaos in my life. I consistently was able to continue the process of grounding my home. Because my home represented such a big stretch for me, it was easy for me to get fearful and create instability, which in turn created chaos that hurt me. Each time this occurred, I knew to go inside to soothe and heal the frightened parts of me.

After the year-long process of creating my home, my loan officer came to one of my workshops. It was fun to hear him share with the others what he had learned from me. He explained to the amusement of the other students that he knew there was something to me and my teachings. He related that he would make ten frustrating attempts to call me or the other people he dealt with before reaching me or them. When I would intend to call him, I would pick up the phone, and without dialing, he would be on the line. He explained that that happened so often he knew what I lived and was attempting to teach him was very powerful and effective. So he shared that he began slowing down and focusing on how to take the chaos and victimization out of his life.

Do you create so chaotically that orderly, successful creation is nearly impossible? . . ❧ . . Do you make ten frustrating calls in your self-created stress, or do you masterfully pick up the phone once and connect immediately? . . ❧ . . Are you willing to explore the possibility that if you slow down, then you will actually have more time and with that time, a greater probability of success?

Breathe! It is amazing what you can create with slow, loving breath.

Pearl Forty-Eight

Creating Loving Support

As the plans were being drawn up for my home, I called the contractor to get some information that I had been promised. The person that I had been assigned to deal with held the phone out a little ways from her mouth and yelled to someone. She referred to me as a nut case and used horrible swear words to describe me. My world had been so free of that kind of violent and abusive language for so long that I questioned what had happened. I had forgotten that people live this way.

After I hung up, I went inside myself to explore if I had some hidden negative feelings about this person or something that I needed to deal with. Nothing really surfaced. I could feel that my preference would have been to love this person even though she had chosen to be abusive to me.

I went to my loan officer to tell him what had happened and asked what I should do. I explained to him that I was not used to people treating me this way. His first question was, "Did you blast her back?" I smiled and explained that was not the way I did business. He mentioned that she was under a lot of stress and was not a bad person. Then he said, "Don't worry. I'll take care of it."

The next week, I got a call from a different lady in the contractor's office. She mentioned that she had been assigned to my job and would be helping me. I went in to see her. Soon we were talking about our love of God and how my house was being created out of my love of God. So as the months went on and many decisions were made concerning my home, I spent much time with this lady. When the project was near completion, she mentioned that she had prayed for my success in creating my home every day since she met me. She knew it was a stretch for me. Sharing our love for God was a beautiful part of the creation of my home.

Had the first lady not vented her frustration at me, I would have missed the chance to enlist the help of a person who was in harmony with my love of God. Don't waste time hating anyone. If you do have negative feelings about someone, then deal with them by releasing them. Once you do, allow your desire to love move you to someone who is more open to appreciating and valuing your ability to love.

Do you fight people who are rude to you? . . . . . If someone is rude, do you endure them and continue to remain in an abusive situation? . . . . . Or do you hold clarity about your desire to love, allowing that to uplift the situation?

Our creative power always gives us what we desire when we are clear. For me, my desire to love created a rich opportunity to both receive and share love from someone who helped me create my home.

•

Pearl Forty-Nine

When Is It Time to Stop Pushing?

As I created my home, I learned that every time I tried to save money, it cost me three times the price. My fear about money would send the prices upward and create pain for me when they did. After this happened on several occasions, I began relaxing and choosing what I loved.

After the loan was approved and the price set for my four thousand square foot home, there were two unexpected twenty-thousand-dollar increases. The first one produced a huge amount of passion on my part, and I didn't give an inch to settle for less in terms of quality or what I desired. Then I created the extra money.

However, when the second twenty-thousand-dollar increase appeared, I handled it differently. By this time, I was tired. My heart and emotions were worn down from so much demand placed upon them. I could feel that my heart wanted to snuggle into my home and not have to push or create more money. I also wanted to focus on my business, which had suffered from having so much of my efforts devoted to creating my home. So when I found out about this last increase, I gave my heart the rest it desired.

I decided to go with a less expensive siding than the stucco that I originally wanted; that decision allowed me to make up the extra money I needed. This was a very good decision. Later I learned that stucco does not work well where I lived and some applications tend to deteriorate quickly. Had I placed it on my home, I would have probably created a long-term problem. My heart loved that I listened to it, freeing it of the burden of creating more money and dealing with delays.

Had I not been able to feel my heart, I might have disregarded it and hurt myself by doing so. By feeling when my heart desired to rest and respecting that, it allowed me to make a wise choice that felt very good.

Is there a creative place in your life where you are weary and tired of driving and pushing? . . . . Are you willing to rest with God and trust? . . . . Do you push yourself into exhaustion or do you allow God to support you in creating your dream? . . . . Do you listen to your heart when it desires to rest and relax?

Only if you learn to listen to your heart will you know how to make the right decisions to help create what you love and support your heart as you do.

Pearl Fifty

Creating What My Heart Loves

Creating what your heart loves transforms your life from drudgery to a life that is joyful and flows easily. When your heart is closed, you create a resistance to what you desire, thereby blocking your natural creative flow. When you open your heart, the impedance drops and an easy flow allows your creativity to support your blessed desires.

For example, I had a student who had worked for about ten years as a maid. Life was hard for her, and she was stuck in every area of her life. In order for her to come into the school, she bartered her maid services for her tuition. In the school, she began learning about loving herself. Within about four months, she found me a new maid. She quit her house-cleaning job and created a well-paying professional job at a university.

Only through her self-love was she able to rise above the limitations of suffering that her mind had imposed upon her. Once she began understanding self-love, she went far beyond this by creating not only a new job, but also a mate and a business she now shares with him. She had the potential all along to create a life of fulfillment, joy, and intimacy. However, until her heart was opened and made important and valuable in her life, she was stuck in a world of labor and loneliness. Her heart now guides her creations and, as a result, takes her into greater fulfillment each day.

I also see this occurring in relationship to an individual's health. A man chose to attend a men's workshop even though he had experienced a heart attack a few months before. Right before the workshop began, his family expressed to me their deep concern that he would die during the workshop; indeed, physically he looked as though he was close to death. I tuned into his condition and confirmed their fear. I responded, "You're right. He is going to die, but I don't know whether he will choose a physical death or a spiritual one. Either way, the sacredness and love that is present in this workshop will deeply support his highest good." I compassionately explained that we would all have to wait to find out his choice and suggested that the family create support for themselves while he attended the men's workshop.

Miraculously, when this man felt the love of the other men, he made the choice to live. After the workshop, his reality rapidly expanded to create what his heart desired. Now he laughs a lot and delights himself with his new life, as he teaches other men how to heal their wounded hearts. And in this state of joy and love, he has chosen to live a very, very long time.

Some of my favorite work is watching when owners of large companies shift their focus from their minds to their hearts. On one trip, a business-owner sent his limousine to the airport for me. His driver excitedly shared that he too was a student, even though he had never attended the school or my self-love classes. Proudly, he explained that his boss was teaching him what he was learning. He shared that his boss had changed in amazing ways, and with these changes, so did his business. The chauffeur soaked up insights from his boss, and his relationship with his wife turned around as a result. He was deeply touched at how close he and his children had become. Smiling, he said, "There is nothing in my life that is the same since my boss met you. It is so important; please don't ever stop teaching."

Once understanding of the heart was introduced into this company, the student ecstatically watched the impact of love on the financial success of his company. Introduction of the heart into the business not only increased profitability but also touched the lives of many.

Is your life burdensome, hard, and unfulfilling? . . ❦. . Are you willing to dissolve your resistance to loving yourself and allow greater love for yourself in your daily life? . . ❦. . Are you willing to create change in your life guided by your open heart? . . ❦. . What would be the first step to create this? . . ❦. . Are you willing to trust taking that step now?

You are the only one who can choose to live what your heart loves. Only the best can come from opening your heart.

Pearl Fifty-One

What My Head Wants, Maybe My Heart Doesn't

I teach a very powerful workshop called *Creating Your Heart's Desire.* In this workshop, the first thing I do is help individuals get in touch with what their hearts desire.

At one workshop, a lady described in long detail how she wanted to expand her business so that she could sell it for a good price. From a previous discussion with her, I knew that she was fed up with her company and wanted nothing further to do with it. When I pointed this out to her, it shocked her. "You're right. I don't even like this business. I want out of it," she honestly shared.

"Then instead of creating what your head is telling you by expanding the business, listen, and tell me what your heart desires," I insisted.

She clearly verbalized, "I want to sell my business." When she got this clarity, the entire class stood up and cheered because they got such a powerful lesson on the difference between creating what their minds believed they were supposed to do versus what their hearts wanted to create.

In another workshop, there was a gifted real estate salesperson who loved her job. As she became more spiritually aware, her mind convinced herself that she should quit her job and do something more service-oriented. I helped her to see that she played an important role in the lives of people. Buying a home is a difficult transition in someone's life, and having a person be there who is loving and focused in her heart helps tremendously. This lady's loving heart assisted others in that way.

Once she freed her mind of the belief that her real estate job was not important as a way to serve her spirituality, she beamed. Her heart was happy that her mind would support her in doing what she loved. Only in feeling her heart's desire and allowing that to be important, did she feel the clarity to stop creating conflict about her career.

When we let our minds alone rule our actions, there is huge resistance and resentment that builds up because we are ignoring our hearts and our true feelings. Our minds perceive they are assisting us by forcing us into patterns and beliefs our parents or society tell us are important. Unfortunately, all that comes out of living without what our hearts' desire is frustration, pain, and resistance. Some individuals spend their entire lives ignoring their hearts and living what their minds believe they are supposed to live. Others eventually destroy the limitations that their minds have imposed upon them, so their hearts' desires can be expressed.

It is through experiencing one's heart that fulfillment is created. If your life is far from expressing what your heart values, you probably sense that your heart is a luxury you cannot afford. This painful reality wastes your life by forcing you to live what you heart does not desire. Once you have enough self-love, this changes; I have seen it over and over. Once your love for yourself increases, you feel clearly what you love, and you can express it. Then you can create what you love rather than what your mind perceives you are supposed to create. It is from this place of creating love within yourself that makes life worth living.

Can you feel what your heart desires? . . . . Are you living this? . . . . If not, are you open to increasing your love for yourself so that you may live what you love?

A wonderful way to begin this process is to let your heart know that you desire to learn how to love yourself more. If you do, you may be surprised at how deeply this touches your heart.

Pearl Fifty-Two

Flying Leaps or Loving Hops

Each of us has our own natural way to create. For me, I would prefer to go without for a longer time in order to get exactly what I want rather than settle for something smaller that I don't want. I have always been like that. I would willingly stay unfulfilled for awhile. However, once I jump into fulfillment, I jump big.

My mind tends to short circuit if my goal is smaller than what I desire. My heart knows what it desires, and if I sense that I am settling for less, my passion disengages and diminishes support for my creation. When I shifted to creating my large dream home, rather than a nice smaller one, my passion fully engaged, even though it was going to be a stretch for me.

I have observed friends who are different. They are so aware of keeping their feeling self happy and content that they prefer taking several smaller steps. That way they get to enjoy each step of the way without putting their emotional self through undo stress.

These friends and I would get frustrated with each other until we learned that each of us has our own way of creating. They might spend hours trying to get me to take on a smaller project so I wouldn't have to do without anything for so long. Then they would get their feelings hurt when I didn't take their advice. I can clearly see how using steps to create what they wanted in small doses kept them from the stressful places that I went to by waiting to take such huge jumps for what I wanted.

Even though I know that creating in big jumps is more difficult, I still tend to make that choice. It flows with my basic nature. I love one good flying leap more than several loving hops.

Feel whether you are a natural flying leaper or loving hopper. If you are a loving hopper and you try to do a flying leap, it creates stress that may work against your success. If you are a flying leaper and you try to do a loving hop, nothing much happens if your passion is not fully engaged. Neither one is good or bad. What is important is that you understand yourself and use that understanding to assist yourself in creating.

Some individuals are good at both, and which pattern they choose is based on the situation or project. Others are strongly polarized into these extremes. If you are comfortable in both areas, then be grateful and learn to apply these different styles in the most advantageous way.

Pearl Fifty-Three

Walking Through My Fear-Limitation Barrier

If you desire to move into a greater expression of yourself, you must walk through your own fear-limitation barrier. This barrier is the resistance that keeps your reality held to its present expression as opposed to what you truly desire and can therefore create.

In other words, the fear-limitation barrier is the internal physical, emotional, mental, and spiritual barriers of resistance and fear if you create beyond a certain level of power or physical expression. If you choose to stretch beyond your normal level of power, you tend to feel uncomfortable because of your fear-limitation barrier.

Like a governor on a motor that allows the motor to operate only up to a certain speed, our fear-limitation barrier holds us to a certain creative power. We have the choice to spend a lifetime below this threshold or be courageous enough to break through it.

When we reach past this barrier, we restructure our physical, emotional, mental, and spiritual selves to support a new level of creativity and power. This choice naturally occurs as we learn to love ourselves more.

Find an area of your life that you would like to expand by freeing yourself from diminished feelings and an inability to live what your heart loves. Try to recognize your fear-limitation barrier. In order to go beyond what you are living now, you must walk through this barrier.

If you realize that this is only a barrier to a greater expression of yourself, then you can love yourself through it. You can use self-love to transform fear into love. That's the easy way. It might sound like this:

I know this is scary. I love myself. Everything is going to be all right. Don't worry. I love myself regardless of whether I get through my fear-limitation barrier or not. I'll always love myself. Let's go through our barrier easily, one step at a time. If I get scared, let me know so I can comfort myself. It's going to be all right. I can slow down if it is too much. Let me hold myself while I walk through my fears. I trust myself. I'm really good at dissolving these fears. I love myself.

Notice how present you can be for yourself with these words. They soothe, comfort, and take the fear out of moving forward.

The other way is to force yourself through your fear-limitation barrier. Unfortunately, the more you force and demand, the more scared and determined you get to keep yourself from growing and expressing what you want. Your inner voice might sounds like this:

Get it right this time, or else I won't ever get what I want. I'll make myself move through this fear. Do it. I've had enough of my puny fears. I'll never get it right. I am fed up with me. I can't stand me disappointing myself one more time. Get through the fears. I'll shut off my feelings so that fear can't stop me. I'll make myself do it.

Chances are very great that not much of anything happens. You may use your will to do it, but forcing with your will only causes your heart to close. This is a great price to pay. The stubborn part of you knows it is locked in fear, and the more you push, the tighter the lock gets.

Some of us learned how to be very harsh with ourselves as children. If we struggled in an area of our life, we were yelled at and told we were inadequate. This type of unloving language keeps us trapped in fear. When our minds which form our language are trained to soothe and encourage us, everything in our feeling worlds begins to relax. It is through relaxation that our true abilities are unlocked, to move us forward to create what we love.

I work with students who are locked in the tight grips of their fear-limitation barriers. The bonds loosen once they learn to sweet-talk themselves out of their fears. Eventually, through loving themselves, their self-love builds to great enough levels that the stubborn denial relaxes enough for self-love to penetrate. Their destiny changes into a new reality, and they succeed at creating what their hearts love.

Feel a fear-limitation barrier that is holding you back. . .✿. .When you try to overcome it, do you push yourself like a demanding, critical drill sergeant who is never satisfied? . .✿. . Are you mean and harsh to yourself?

Practice encouraging yourself with gentle, sweet, and non-demanding words to walk through your fear-limitation barrier. Notice the effect on your body of this gentle, nonthreatening approach.

Pearl Fifty-Four

Clutter, Chaos, and Change

My teachings cause very rapid change in students' lives. If they manifest the change in an orderly fashion, then the individuals greatly increase their probability of success in creating what they love. If they manifest the change in a disorderly fashion, then it creates chaos. So I work with my students to teach them how to create change with the least amount of disruption and chaos in their lives.

I'll share with you my teachings. If you are going through a big shift or transition, it is essential that you slow down. Using your mind to push yourself faster than your naturally slow emotional body can handle creates chaos that overloads you. Working faster actually works against you. The students are instructed to create time and awareness to stay in touch with their feelings, while they are involved with a big transformation or creating a difficult manifestation.

Be impeccably clean, clear, and together. Your internal world of emotions and thoughts are perfectly expressed by your external world. If clutter and trash fills your home, office, or car, then I can guarantee that your internal world has similar chaos. Your mind and emotions get scattered, confused, and jammed through an array of unorganized thoughts and emotions. Once you get lost in this clutter, you won't know the old, more closed you from the new, open you. This can create wasted focus and dispersed creative power. With enough chaos and clutter you soon feel as though you are on a gerbil wheel going nowhere while expending huge amounts of energy.

There is an easier way. When I was creating my home, I always knew to have my van washed before seeing my loan officer. I wanted my mind and emotions as clear and free of stress and clutter as possible. During this time, I carefully monitored my environment for a buildup of clutter. If clutter formed, I knew it was a warning that I was going too fast or not maintaining the stability necessary to create what my heart desired.

One of the techniques I use now to maintain that stability is to daily empty the trash in my office. When I do this, it leaves my environment free of the old and unused information, settled, and clear for hours before the new creations enter the next day.

This simple act tells my mind and body that maintaining a clear, uncluttered flow is important to me, and I have a procedure to assure that it is done both internally and externally. Through removing what is old and unnecessary, my heart is free to relax and feel an uncluttered mind that supports what my heart loves.

Survey your environments such as your home, office, and car. Are they harmonious environments? . . . . Or are they reflections of chaos and clutter? . . . . If they are chaotic, can you feel your internal chaos that creates the external chaos? . . . . Are you willing to slow down and restore harmony in your internal physical, emotional, mental, and spiritual selves that create your external environment?

Rapid change occurs most easily and positively when the old is naturally removed while maintaining order and cleanliness. If you create this, you will find your heart will love this pattern because it assists in feeling safe and supported to enter your new, more positive, reality.

Pearl Fifty-Five

Creating a Car I Love

On the way to teaching one of my workshops, *Creating Your Heart's Desire,* I realized how much my van meant to me after driving it for seven years. I was very aware when I created it, and I knew God was guiding me. Buying a van would have never occurred to me otherwise, because I'm not the van type, and I never desired or even thought about one.

When it was time for me to give up my home and quit my engineering job seven years earlier, I received very clear intuitive guidance to buy a van. After my initial disappointment that a van was in my best interest, I purchased a new one. I was entering into a period in my life when I would have little security. I knew that the most important thing to me about this van was that it was safe, reliable, and maintenance-free.

As I drove to the workshop, my heart was almost bursting with gratitude for my van. It had been there consistently for me through difficult and long-term transformations. Moving eight times, teaching seminars everywhere, traveling, and living my spiritual work and life had all been possible with my van's support. Many memories included my van. Through one-hundred and thirty-seven thousand miles of travel, my van had been safe and reliable. I loved the van for having provided that consistent sense of security.

My love of the van was so strong that I could understand why I had resisted purchasing a new vehicle for several years. I could sense that I needed to make peace with how much I valued my van for having supported me in this way. Also, before I was willing to create a new vehicle, I needed to trust that I could transfer that safety and reliability onto a new car. Until I did these things, my motivation was low to replace my van.

During this particular workshop, I let my heart celebrate my love for my van creation, which had provided security for me for seven years. I went deep inside to feel what my heart desired for my next creation. I had loved the safety, security, and reliability so much that I knew I would transfer that way of loving myself directly into my next vehicle.

I could feel how much I had grown and matured in those seven years. I was no longer jobless and without owning a home. My world had totally transformed as a result of the courage I had to leap into the unknown.

My heart was exploring two types of vehicles. One vehicle was playful and fun, and one represented my ability to create what I loved on the physical level. By the end of the workshop, my heart was very clear. It was ready to bring the power in to create the car that I really desired. I knew that with this more practical car, the play would naturally follow.

The next week, I bought my car which represented to me the power to create what I love. By then I had deeply and completely released my van. Profound changes immediately came into my life the day I released my van and moved into my next creation. I was ready for this next step and fully aware of what I was creating.

What did you create your car to be? . . ❧ . . Is it safe, reliable, pleasurable, sporty, supportive, or whatever else you wanted? . . ❧ . . If you are displeased with what you have created, then you must be willing to honestly feel the intentions behind your creation and adjust them if they do not please your heart.

For me, my creations are not objects isolated from me. My creations such as my car, home, and career are fully connected expressions of my ability to love myself and create what I love with God. Each creation represents within me an expression of myself as I allow God's love to bless and help me create what I love. This is a rich way to live because my creations are fully infused with God's love. So open your heart, allow your creations to be expressions of what your heart desires, and infuse them with God's love.

Pearl Fifty-Six

How Distrust Can Keep Me from My Heart's Desire

As I teach people to create their hearts' desires, the biggest danger to them—of getting less than what they love or nothing at all—is using the pattern of distrust.

Let's say that a man clearly feels what his heart wants to create. His feeling of desire is tangible, and every cell in his body lets him know how pleasing this creation is to his heart. As he feels his love for this creative project, his passion builds. He is more alive, loving, and full than normal. I know that if he continues holding true to these feelings within himself, his dream will become his reality.

But suddenly, out of nowhere, his mind starts questioning if he made the right choice. Perhaps he should choose a different project. Maybe he didn't really want to own his own home now. His present job isn't so bad—stressful, low paying, and demanding—but if he tries harder maybe he can endure it until he retires in thirty years.

One moment he has a true, tangible feeling of what would bring great joy, and he rapidly builds the momentum necessary to make it his. The next moment his mind is questioning this desire, and his momentum fizzles.

This happens because he gets scared as he begins walking through his fear-limitation barrier. The minute fear sets in, he begins distrusting his deep-heart knowing. If he doesn't quickly stop the questioning and fear, then his dream collapses like a house of cards.

When you have a deep-heart knowing, write it down clearly. Write down the feelings that let you know that this is truly your heart's desire so that you can reread it if your mind starts doubting. If you can remember the heart feeling that let you know this project was for you, then you can create your heart's desire more easily.

I remember the instant my heart told me it wanted a 4,000 square foot home. During the process of building my home, when I got scared or it looked like there was no hope, I remembered that my heart desired this and was helping me to create it. Then I would calm down. When your mind starts questioning your selections, your timing, or your desires, you can reread or remember your knowing about what your heart truly desires.

When this level of fear is present, it can be debilitating because everything appears to support the fear. When I sensed that my mind was sabotaging my creation through questioning, I clearly identified this pattern. As I did this, I talked to myself to begin the process of calming myself down. I navigated through my fear by identifying it and recognizing it for what it was. I calmed myself by repeating the following dialogue:

I know I'm scared, Sweetie. It's going to be okay. I'm questioning my dream because I'm scared. Don't worry. Everything is going to be all right. Let's stop the questioning and relax. Okay? Trust. I love myself. I trust myself. Don't worry, it's going to be all right.

By this time, perhaps I worry that by questioning my creation, I might louse it up and have something new to fear. Then I could affirm:

Don't worry. God gives me lots of grace when I create. If I slip a little bit, God's grace takes care of it. Everything will be fine. Don't worry. Trust.

What if my fear creates concern that I slipped too much for recovery. Then I can say:

I love myself so much. My love is very powerful. My love is even more powerful than slipping a whole bunch. Don't worry. God's love is taking care of everything. Trust. Everything is going to be all right. I love myself. I love my creation.

If you have a pattern of questioning and distrusting your creations, then mark this page for yourself. The next time you try to sabotage your heart's project by creating fear, slowly and very lovingly read the above dialogue to yourself. As you get the feeling of it, say what you need to hear to calm down. Walk through your fear-limitation barrier with your heart open and allow your dream to become grounded.

Parents and the Heart

Pearl Fifty-Seven

Hurt, Healing, and Children

My son's life was amazingly easy for his first four years. Nicknamed Sunshine at his nursery school, he trusted wholeheartedly that life was good and felt a bright enthusiasm and love in all that he created. As his father and I began the divorce process, however, a difficult and painful cloud overshadowed him.

Before the divorce, when I would pick him up from nursery school, he would hop into my car full of enthusiasm and joy from his day. He could not wait to share his adventures and was excited about going home to create new ones.

Suddenly, his world made no sense to him, and he would cry and fight every time I arrived to pick him up. The distress and fighting would begin as he was forced to get into the car and continued long after we arrived home. I could not live long like this. It was too painful for both of us.

I knew he was in deep pain, yet there had to be a better way of expressing and dealing with it. After praying for help, I had an idea. We would have a happy contest when I picked him up. I explained the rules of the happy contest to him—who could name the most experiences that caused us to feel happy during the day—and within a few days, the destructive cloud associated with our rides home disappeared. This helped my son to focus on creating positive experiences in the midst of the pain of the divorce.

In order to give him tools to deal with his pain, I began telling him stories about a bunny who happened to be going through similar experiences. I could tell his heart hung onto every word about this bunny. He would adjust my story or have me repeat a part if he felt it was important in terms of understanding the bunny and his many feelings. Sometimes, he would tell part of the story. We both learned that through the stories, he could express and share his concerns which he might not have felt safe to do otherwise. We both knew who the bunny was.

When I felt that my son was building up anger, which was the result of his pain, I would suggest that he pound a pillow to release it. He was unwilling to do this. However, if I felt the anger was building, I would tell him that I felt too much anger in our home, and that I was going to help get rid of it. I would ask him to watch.

Verbally expressing what I was feeling, I would pound the pillow against the bed as I released my anger, as well as his. He would eventually laugh, and I then knew that I had helped him to release the anger that was hurting both of us.

One time, he agreed to release his anger with the pillow, but he touched such deep anger that it frightened him. He was afraid of this much rage, and I could never again encourage him to face it directly with a pillow. Later he learned to use exercise and movement as less frightening ways of dealing with anger.

Deep laughter is another powerful, enjoyable way to deal with negative emotions. It is as effective as crying or yelling in terms of moving destructive emotions. I would use a comforter to roll my son up like a worm, leaving only his head free. Then, I would tickle him. We both loved to do this, and it was a powerful part of our play. We never tired of doing this. Fair is fair, however, so after my son finished his cathartic laughter, I would be rolled up like a worm for my laughter. Much healing, as well as play, took place with this exercise. After we finished, our hearts would be wide open and free of pain.

Are you using your creative self to support your child learning to deal with his or her anger and hurt feelings? . . ❧✿☙ . . Or are you stuck in fear and control in terms of relating to your loved ones?

Your heart has many powerful keys to transform painful situations into joyful experiences. This is a tremendous gift to yourself and your child if you learn to use these keys.

Pearl Fifty-Eight

The Rocking Chair and the Heart

One of the most magical parts of being a parent to my son was the rose-colored, stuffed rocking chair. We used it for a ritual that both our hearts treasured. He would rest in my lap, legs dangling over the edge of the chair. In the rocking chair, he always set the tone of our time together. Sometimes, he would be as mature as any adult; other times, he would be as immature and babyish as he desired. Any choice that satisfied his heart or emotions was acceptable in the rocking chair.

Our ritual always began with my singing the same lullaby song and transitioning this into a song about my son. The song related to his situation, whether he was struggling or experiencing something wonderful. He could not wait to hear the magical expressions about himself in these songs.

I never had to wonder about how much this meant to him. Many times I heard him tell his friends, "My mom is the best singer in the world. She sings to me." Much as his love of my singing meant to me, however, I knew that he was really referring to the richness of the heart that came through my songs. I had been an emotionally damaged child, and I had not sung prior to this. Although I would have loved to have provided tonal quality, it was not possible at that time of my life.

As I sang to my son, my musical ability reopened. I began writing songs and wanted to introduce the new lullabies into our time together. My son absolutely refused. He loved the ritual the way it was and wanted our heart time to stay that way forever—and so it did.

After singing, we would talk and play silly games. Sometimes, if he got too funny or playful, I would roll him to the ground and pretend he was too much for me. Always, it was creative and playful, and we loved it.

Upon his return from school one evening, my son was upset and kicked me. He had never done this before, and I was uncertain about how to handle it. I told him to go to his room and explained that hurting me was not okay. This heightened his distress. He yelled, "I'm going to run away forever and never speak to you again!" I went to the rocking chair, sat down, and began focusing on how much I loved him. As I sat loving him, feeling more and more love and golden light, he went to his room to pack. I could hear his toys and treasures being tossed and moved around.

Soon, he stood in my doorway. He repeated, "I'm leaving forever and never speaking to you again." I told him I understood that this was a difficult choice that he felt he must make. Then, I returned to loving him, and within a few minutes, he was in my lap. The moment he laid down, he burst into tears and said the children had made fun of him at school. His heart did not know how to deal with the pain of it. I soothed and comforted him as he cried. He never again kicked me or packed to run away.

I released our rocking chair rituals when my son was ten in order to allow him to mature. I cried for hours about giving up the magical experience but knew that my heart had to find new avenues to express this love and creativity as my son stepped into the next phase of his life. Perhaps, we will share this magic with his children one day.

Have you created heart rituals with your children that open both you and your child's hearts? . . ❦ . . Do you have a safe environment, such as a rocking chair, where your child can be either mature or very immature, depending on his or her inner needs with you there to support? . . ❦ . . Do you allow your heart to create something magical and rich with your child?

Life can be beautiful and warm even in the midst of challenging life experiences and lessons. Our heart and creative selves have the ability to bring a magical, loving presence into whatever we are living, no matter how seemingly difficult. Truly, it is a choice worth making.

Pearl Fifty-Nine

The Easy Way to Quit Thumb-Sucking

My son stopped his occasional thumb-sucking around the age of two. With the trauma of the divorce when he was four, he resumed the habit. I never said anything about it.

The night before his seventh birthday, I had the following discussion with him. I explained that the next day he would be seven, and that I felt that was a very mature age. He smiled proudly as he agreed with me. I suggested that he feel inside himself to see if he wanted to continue sucking his thumb, since he would be so mature.

I also shared with him that our birthday is a very powerful day, and it is a day that we can create our dreams coming true. I suggested that if he was ready as a seven-year-old to give up this habit, his birthday would be the perfect time to create a new pattern.

We never talked about it again, nor did I ever see him suck his thumb after this. Obviously, he felt inside and found it very natural and easy to release that pattern.

Do you empower your child and respect his or her choices? . . . Or do you attempt to force your children to live according to your beliefs and desires? . . . When you create an environment in which your child learns to feel what he or she desires, you empower trust in his or her inner knowing. With your supportive confidence in his or her choice, you teach your child to trust his or her ability to create it. The result of this type of parenting is an empowered child confident of making loving choices with an ability to manifest these choices into his or her daily life. What a rich treasure to gift your child!

Pearl Sixty

Dealing with Fear

Before my husband and I got a divorce, our four-year-old son did not know what fear was. As the divorce began, his secure world was turned upside down. He became terrified of most children's cartoons and was especially afraid of toy guns. I subsequently screened all his television shows in a futile attempt to protect him and to reduce fear in his world. His viewing options got smaller and smaller, yet his panic intensified. Additionally, I had always discouraged him from playing with guns because of my distaste for violence. Once fear entered his world, guns seemed to especially upset and terrorize him.

One day, his four-year-old friend was playing with a toy water pistol. He pointed it at my son, chased him, and sprayed water on him. My son ran into our home terrified and incapacitated by his fear. His panic shocked me. I suddenly realized I had been feeding his fear and giving validity to it. I could no longer participate in "protecting my son," which was debilitating and victimizing him.

My dislike for violence and guns had created an obsessive fear within him. Likewise, screening his television programs was creating more and more fearful responses. Without realizing it, I was validating his fear that this is an unsafe world. In a very fundamental way, my approach was creating the opposite result of what I desired.

I asked my son to come with me to the store. On the way, I said, "I realize that, in the past, things like guns and television frightened you. However, I sense that you have matured so much that you can handle things that were previously difficult for you." He looked at me curiously.

At the toy store, I found the water pistols and asked him to choose one that he liked. He protested, "But mom, I'm not supposed to like guns." I replied, "Since you are so mature and can handle things so well, I thought that a water pistol would be fun. What do you think?" He agreed and rapidly selected one. I chose one too.

We went home and filled our water guns. Within moments, he was running around having a great time squirting me and the young neighbor kid who had incapacitated him with fear less than an hour earlier.

I told him that since he was doing so well dealing with his fear, I would no longer screen his cartoons. I was confident that he would make good choices and could handle whatever he saw. And so he did.

Look inside your life. Do you validate fear for yourself and/or those you love by trying to protect against it? . . ✿ . . If you trusted yourself or others to handle fear, what difference would this make? . . ✿ . . Are you willing to make this leap forward?

Fear is as real as we make it. True protection teaches us that we have the power to deal with our fear. As we learn how to go beyond our fear, we free ourselves of painful limitation.

· Pearl Sixty-One

A Mother's Sleeping Child

Moonlight snuggles around my sleeping child,
Caressing him with silver shadowy nurturing peace.
My heart celebrates a sacred ceremony, ancient as time.
Love reveries of a mother, watching her sleeping child.

Waves of expanding love rising from deep within,
Ever increasing for this beautiful child,
Pushing warm tears aside, grateful for their release.
Love reveries of a mother, watching her sleeping child.

Sweetness softly singing of a heart at peace,
Too soon he must carry the burden of a troubled world,
Too soon his love to be tested by those not worthy.
Love reveries of a mother, watching her sleeping child.

No angel more holy than this dreaming child,
Protect him, God, surround your most sacred treasure
Allowing his heart to be free.
Love reveries of a mother, watching her sleeping child.

If only all could feel this love, peace would enwrap our Earth.
For who then would dare send a soldier to battle,
Knowing each one was a mother's sleeping child.
Love reveries of a mother, watching her sleeping child.

When we feel this level of profound love for our children, we may perceive that it is our job to provide love for these precious beings forever. Certainly, loving them deeply is part of the magic and joy of being parents, but there is an important step beyond this.

The greatest gift we can give our children is to teach them by example to love themselves. As they learn to provide abundant love for themselves, they escape the debilitating patterns of codependency and low self-esteem that are created by not knowing how to provide love for themselves and by perceiving that they are dependent and needy of the love and approval of others.

We can teach children from infancy that they are lovable and to connect to love so profoundly that the richness they experience through the love of a parent is accessible to them with or without this parent. With this profound connection to love, they are freed of disempowerment and inability to create love in their life.

A wonderful way that children learn to love themselves deeply is to have them to feel the love they have for an animal. When they are feeling this pure and great love for their animals, ask them to focus on the same profound love for themselves. When they are hurting, when things are not working well for them, or when things are going wondrously well, we can guide them through this exercise of self-love which, in truth, connects them to God as love.

Are you open to teaching your children to love themselves? . . 🌹 . . Or are you afraid that if they know how to love themselves, they will not need you? . . 🌹 . . Are you willing to trust that teaching your child self-love will actually increase the love between you and your child?

The quality of life your children will be able to create through learning self-love is infinitely greater than if they miss this rich life lesson.

Pearl Sixty-Two

Children Driving You Crazy?

This is a jewel. When your children are wild and a bit out of control, family rebellion is often at play. Rebellion cannot exist in the presence of acceptance because rebellion is always in opposition to something. Fighting or resisting rebellion only gives it more power.

When things get wound up and out of control, say the following affirmation, and if the kids are old enough, have them say it with you. This affirmation literally removes rebellion from your reality:

Rebellion has no time, space, or authority in our world.

Often, this will serve as a calming balm on the entire situation. You may think it works because the children say the affirmation. The truth is that your rebellion was feeding directly into the children who were acting it out. That's why I called it family rebellion. When anyone in the family moves their rebellion, it is amazing how the entire dynamics shift to something more connected, successful, and peaceful.

If you teach your children this affirmation and how to identify rebellion without negative judgment on it, you will be giving your children a great gift. When your young ones reach their teenage years, they will have reduced their desire for rebellion and learned how to deal with it in a constructive and loving way. The best will come of this.

Notice if you hate this affirmation and are concerned that it will deny your children their identity. If so, chances are that you have deeply embedded rebellion yourself. You probably believe that the only way you can be safe is to rebel. In truth, rebellion pushes away love, true empowerment, and self-confidence.

Rebellion ensures isolation, loneliness, and inability to create what you love. If you are ready to heal, you might want to say this affirmation often until you are satisfied with the results. Be prepared to feel and experience more love, connection, and being valued than you have probably ever experienced. Also, be prepared to feel closer to your children than you ever have.

Are you loyal to rebellion and feel that it is the only way to be safe? . .❧. . Do you like it when your children rebel? . .❧. . Are you willing to walk out of your loyalty to rebellion?

As family rebellion is uplifted, it is natural for peace, harmony, and unity to replace the chaos and disruptiveness.

Pearl Sixty-Three

When My Child Wants to Do Something that Hurts Me

If your child desires to do something that makes your skin crawl, there are ways to handle it while maintaining a relationship of love and mutual respect between you and your child. This worked consistently for me with my son who is now grown and in college. Recently, I asked him how he felt about the way I handled these situations and he replied, "Mom, I feel good about it. You never gave me rules, and you never told me I couldn't do what I wanted to do."

One day, he announced that he was having his ear pierced. I suggested that before he did so, he should survey classmates who had their ears pierced and those who didn't. I asked that he then look deeply inside himself and choose which group best portrayed the image he felt was most appropriate for him. That was the last time he ever mentioned it.

I assume he felt that the image that best fit him did not have pierced ears. Had he chosen to have his ear pierced, I would have trusted that he had made the best decision for himself through careful research and heart searching. I would have accepted his choice.

I loved my son's beautiful well-groomed blonde hair. When he was about ten years old, he announced that he wanted a spike haircut. "What is a spike haircut?" I asked. Horror rippled through my body as he pointed to a youngster who looked like everything I didn't want my son to be. I was appalled at the practically shaved hair that stood out like spikes, as the name implied.

I went deeply into my heart to find an answer. I explained to him that I felt it was important that he express himself with the haircut of his choice, yet what he was choosing would be shocking to me. I asked if he was willing to gradually move into his spike haircut rather than doing it all at once, and he agreed. Over the next several months the beautician took him step-by-step to a full spike hairdo. By the time he got there, the shock was over, and I easily flowed with it.

I've always sensed that he felt closer to me as a result of my asking him to do it in this way. Through this, we both discovered that even if he makes choices that might not be my choice, we would be able to work it out in a way that did not jeopardize or violate our love. Parents, this is powerful medicine!

On another occasion, my son really wanted to go to a party that I felt could have drugs or other abuses present. When he got upset that I would not let him go, he passionately explained to me that he was trustworthy and that I was being unreasonable. He had such strong feelings about this, I suggested that we each draw three cards from a Tarot deck to see the energies behind both our responses. I will always remember the results of this.

My son drew three cards; the Sun, the Star, and Good Fortune. Everything about his desire to go to the party was protected, blessed and pure.

I, on the other hand, drew three miserable cards of fear, death, and loss. I shared with my son that obviously fear caused me to not trust him. I took him to the party. When I returned, he was playing basketball and had obviously lived true to his integrity.

This was a powerful lesson for me. Had I refused to allow him to go, it would have created the sense I did not trust him. I was grateful I did not let my fear create separation and distrust between us.

How do you deal with and respect your child's creative abilities, choices, and desire to create his or her own life? . . 🌹 . . Do you respect your child or do you attempt to force your will and desires upon your child? . . 🌹 . . Do you use force and will to prevent your child from creating what she or he desires, or do you create an environment of love and then trust your child's choices?

When you respect your children's desires while assisting them in defining appropriate self-loving structure, you teach your children to be empowered, confident, and capable of creating whatever they love. This is a great blessing for both you and your child.

Pearl Sixty-Four

Children's Desire to Hurt Themselves

When I arrived home one day, my son was in a rage. He had locked himself out and as a result, missed attending something that was important to him. Raising his hand as if to strike the right side of his head, he exclaimed, "Mom, I was so angry at myself I wanted to hit myself on the head with a stick!" His desire to hurt himself was so strong that I started to tell him that he needed to clear or neutralize it, so that he would not create pain. Unfortunately, I got distracted in my desire to calm him down and never verbalized this to him.

The next day, he had an appointment to get his hair cut. When he came home, part of his head looked as though it had been shaved. Upset, he explained that the beautician was using clippers with a long guard on them to leave several inches of hair, but the guard fell off. Without the guard, she shaved part of his head like a runaway lawn mover. Guess where? The guard fell off at the exact spot where he had aimed at his head with an imaginary stick the preceding day.

Horrified at what she had done, the beautician stayed upset about this for days. My son did not share with her that he had actually used her to play out his desire to hit himself on the head with a stick. She had unknowingly participated in his creation. For the next several weeks, one could literally see the shaved impression of a stick as it would have impacted flat on my son's head had he actually hit himself.

Recovering from the initial shock, I discussed with him my concern when he demonstrated such a strong desire to hurt himself. After he learned the lesson of the power of self-destructive thoughts and desires to hurt himself, I invited him to share his manifestation at one of my classes. It was a beautiful lesson for everyone.

Had I not been distracted at that time, I would have suggested the following for my son to neutralize his destructive desire. While remembering his rage-driven feeling to hurt himself, he could imagine the stick transforming into something like a feather. As he remembered the hurt-filled desire, he could keep discharging the negative charge until he desired to tickle himself with the feather instead of hurting himself.

When discharging destructive desires, it is important to harmlessly discharge the negative feelings as well as to dissolve or neutralize the instrument of hurt into something harmless and insignificant. The stick, for example, could have been made so small in his mind that it would be like a fleck that had no ability to hurt anything.

Do you realize how powerfully creative your destructive thoughts and desires are? . . ❦❦❦ . . When they occur, do you consciously neutralize them, or leave them to create something to hurt you? . . ❦❦❦ . . Are you willing to develop self-love to stop the pain of victimization that comes from self-destructive desires?

Self-love is the powerful creative force that dissolves and heals painful and destructive creative desires.

Pearl Sixty-Five

Rebellion Day

For students who have repressed their rebellion, I suggest rebellion day every once in a while. One of the patterns that I see concerns adults who appear as though they don't have rebellion as an issue, but their children are out of control with rebellion. This triggers an immediate alert for me. The fact is if you do not deal with your rebellion as a parent, your children will play it out for you.

The laws of physics cause the energy to have to go somewhere. If you are keeping a tight grip on rebellion in your own life, then it transfers over to your children. They haven't learned yet how to get a grip on it, so they play it out fully to the shock and horror of the parents and often to their own detriment. This type of pattern can go through many generations before someone in the lineage discharges it through his or her body and bursts the bubble of family rebellion.

If you decide to have a rebellion day, here are my suggestions. Let everyone in your family know that you are rebelling for a set number of hours, and that you are inviting your family members to join you if they like. Explain that the only rules that apply during rebellion day are that nothing is done to hurt anyone or anything, including yourself.

It may surprise you that once you have permission to rebel that the desire to do so collapses. Accepting rebellion collapses its destructive impact. That is the reason you have rebellion day. As you sense rebellion hurting you, you start trying to suppress it. The more you suppress rebellion, the more it grips you. The suppressed rebellion has to go somewhere, and it typically uses your children as an outlet. It is easier to move rebellion out of your internal world so that it simply does not exist inside you any more. You will be amazed at the impact of this on your rebellious children.

One mother I knew encouraged her daughter to wear inappropriate clothing to the local country club. Through her approval and encouragement of her daughter's inappropriate behavior, she was obviously rewarding her daughter for rebelling.

Because she had not healed her own rebellion, she was using her daughter to play out and express it. I'm certain she was unaware of the pain this rebellion would create for her daughter. With this type of rebellion, her daughter would not be able to connect on a heart-level to others, but instead would create being isolated and unable to fit in anywhere.

Do you tend to value rebellion and reward your children for supporting it? . . ❦ . . Do you feel safe with rebellion or do you realize that rebellion actually separates you from your ability to receive love? . . ❦ . . Are you willing to give up your rebellion?

Resolving your rebellion helps free your children of rebellion that can create chaos and an inability for them to connect. The best for you and your children comes from doing this.

Pearl Sixty-Six

Guilt, Parents, and Children

When I teach five-day intensives, parents from out of town are required to be away from their children during this time. At the outset, this provided the opportunity to study guilt, parents, and children. After this, I learned how to quickly help parents struggling with this move into new patterns to free both themselves and their children from guilt.

Parents, most often mothers, would come to the intensives and feel guilty about leaving their children. Within a day, their previously healthy children would develop a fever and vomiting. The only time their children would do this was when a parent left to do something she or he loved to do.

The calls from home would pressure the parents to abandon the learning that was designed to uplift the entire family; and they would rush home to take care of their sick children. I noticed that if the parent agreed to go home, the children soon felt fine. Once the parent arrived home, the children would act as though everything was okay. After this occurred several times, I knew that there were patterns at play that were hurting everyone.

These parents learned from their own parents to experience guilt any time they created something that they truly loved. They had been taught to use their children to hold back their self-expression and creativity. This created unhappiness for the parents and the children. As the parents examined their feelings, they recognized that they did not want their children to feel safe and happy unless they were there. The more painful their role as a parent was, and the more they sacrificed to show their love, the more validated they felt as a loving parent. This validation came from the neediness their children felt for them, a neediness so powerful that, in less than twenty-four hours, it consistently made healthy children sick.

The effect on the children was tortuous. Their choice was to be needy and dependent on their parents. In addition, they were required to display illness and other trauma when their parents were not codependently glued to them, especially if their parents were expressing their own creativity. The children were taught that unless they played that role for their parents, they would not be experiencing love as their family defined love.

I helped the parents to create healthier patterns where the children were rewarded for feeling whole and capable whether the parents were there or not. If they had not healed these patterns, their children would eventually transfer these patterns to their children.

My students learned to identify when they were creating guilt and codependency by the feedback from their children. When the children were needy, the parents knew that on some level, they were influencing their children to play this role. The parents learned to shift that part of themselves that was creating the dependency. As soon as they did, their children could relax, have a great time with carefully chosen sitters, and create a life that worked well for them whether their parent was present or not.

Review your family life. Do you need family members to be needy and unhealthy, preventing you from doing what your heart loves in order to feel that you have value and are loved? . . ❧ . . Are you willing to shift these patterns to ones where everyone can feel empowered and whole whether you are together or not? . . ❧ . . Do you associate love with guilt? . . ❧ . . Does this association really work for you, or is it simply what you learned as a child? . . ❧ . . Do you want to pass this on to your children, or are you ready to heal it for your family?

Children have the right to feel safe, loved, and supported both when their parents are present and when their parents are absent. Parents who deal with their guilt, free children from dysfunctional relationships with their parents. Great blessings come to both the parents and children for doing this.

Pearl Sixty-Seven

Naughty Words

I handled naughty words differently than most moms. When my son was about four years old, I walked into his room as he was struggling to open his closet door. "Oh, shat. Shat!" he exclaimed. "What is '*Oh, shat?*'" I asked, as though I didn't know what he thought he was saying. "Mom, you know. I'm not supposed to say it," he innocently replied, as though he was beyond saying the word he actually intended.

When he was about six years old, I informed him that words can be used to hurt, and that I was greatly opposed to that. If he used words to hurt, whether they were swear words or regular words, I would always be concerned about that and would seek ways to prevent it.

I explained that if he used swear words at school or around most adults while he was a child, the adults would tend to be offended and have a negative response in most cases. If they were in a leadership role with him, for example, in Scouts, church, school, or as parents of his friends, they might seek to punish or ostracize him, which would hurt him.

I explained that if he was hurt by a negative response from an adult, it would upset me because I always wanted the best for him and did not like to feel him in pain. So I suggested that he not use naughty words around adults.

I further explained that if he directed swear words or carefully chosen regular words at another person in anger or used them to hurt, it would create pain, and I was opposed to that also. I advised him that although I was not telling him he couldn't use naughty words, he must understand that it would never be all right to direct them at me or anyone he loved because such words would hurt very deeply.

Many times, I heard my son brag to his friends that I was a special mom because I let him say naughty words. This truly was significant to my son. As a young adult, he still associates this with being special and loved. He never directed any naughty words at me, and as far as I know, he never offended any adults.

As a parent, you have the opportunity to create a structure that works well for both you and your child. If hearing a naughty word offends you, then you would need to modify the above instructions so that your child knows not to say these words in your presence. The important thing is that you develop a loving structure that works for both of you.

I help adults heal the damage done by parents who did not understand the principles of love. Washing your child's mouth out with soap, an abusive process done by parents of my generation, leaves deep scars that your child is bad, dirty, and unworthy of love. Usually this type of punishment will throw children into rebellion and defiance. There are better ways that leave both you and your child mutually loving and respectful. The above approach worked well for my son and me.

In order to set up a structure that supports both you and your child's hearts, you must feel with your heart what works for you and what doesn't. Relying on what you have heard or been taught simply will not give you the tools you need to create something that is truly supportive. Unless it is true to your heart, it is simply a "should" that is based on guilt.

When you learn to become deeply aware of your heart, these feelings will carefully guide you. For example, I was not concerned by naughty words per se. However, I would have been deeply concerned if another adult had attacked or punished my son. Had my heart been offended by his naughty words, then I would have taken an entirely different approach.

When you set up structure with your children, do you do it based on what you were taught or feel you are supposed to do? . . .🌹. . Or do you deeply feel what is real and right for you?

My approach was profoundly different from how my parents dealt with this issue. By my willingness to be true to my heart as well as my son's, I was able to set up a protocol that worked for both of us. This was an important ingredient in how we loved each other. He values my approach to this day.

Too Much, Too Fast

Pearl Sixty-Eight

When Things Are Too Fast, Use Slow-Down Time

Einstein's explanation about the relativity of time was that time with a pretty girl goes by quickly, while time doing something you do not enjoy moves very slowly. Bring to mind examples when you feel that you do not have enough time. See if you can feel the hype that pushes and pushes as your mind tells you that you must do more and more, faster and faster.

This hype-faster-faster program literally compresses time and races reality to Einstein's curve that shows that time compresses as something moves closer to the speed of light.

It is much like a gerbil on a spinning wheel. The faster the wheel goes, the more the gerbil senses that he has to run faster and faster or else his reality will collapse. He is actually correct that the hype-faster-faster reality will collapse by his choice to slow down or get off the wheel.

The gerbil probably senses that by keeping the hype-faster-faster reality going, he is doing some great thing. Yet, if you look at it from the outside, the gerbil is going nowhere faster and faster. Other than the exercise value and satisfying the boredom of an overactive mind, the gerbil is spinning his wheels and will eventually exhaust himself or create boredom from the intensity of the hype-faster-faster program. Are you on a similar gerbil wheel spinning by overdoing faster and faster?

For those of you ready to get off of the gerbil wheel or ready to slow the wheel down, here's what to do. When you have what you perceive as the least amount of time, you *consciously slow everything down.* You walk to the bathroom twice as slowly as normal. You pick up the pencil more slowly. You smell your coffee and breathe deeply to determine if you need caffeine to keep the hype-faster-faster wheel going.

If too many action items need to be dealt with too fast, take a self-loving walk around your business, then come back and choose a few actions that will make the biggest impact. Release the rest of the pile to God and ask that the universe restructure to allow you to slow down and do an even better job at work with less effort.

If you do this, within hours, you will be getting calls canceling the huge list of action items that are there to keep your wheel in hype-faster-faster gear. Or no one will seem to care or notice that these actions aren't addressed. As the desire that created them to perpetuate and justify your hype-faster-faster program collapses inside you, so do the excessive assignments.

What you probably don't realize is that you created all the action items to stay in hype-faster-faster gear. In truth, you are the only one who can choose to slow down time and end the addiction to this pattern.

Only you know why you choose the hype-faster-faster gear. Perhaps you want to appear important, desire to be indispensable, want to go faster and faster to run away from your feelings of pain and life problems, or maybe you want to be like others who are in hype-faster-faster drive.

For hype-faster-faster beings, I know that your minds will tell you terrible things will happen if you slow down. The truth is that your setting for time will slow down; your accuracy and efficiency will increase; your energy level will take you out of hype-depletion and begin the rebuilding process to eliminate depleting your body, heart, and soul; and you will get to smell the roses and enjoy life.

Once the hype-faster-faster reality starts collapsing, you can slow everything down to create what you love in a way that you don't miss a moment of life. When you do, you know you are entering into creating a reality of the heart which provides more with less—less effort, less stress, and less hardship.

Are you addicted to pushing time faster and faster? . . . . Do you believe this is real or do you realize this is simply what you knew how to create? . . . . Does it work for you, or is it creating tremendous stress and depletion?. .❦. . Are you open to slowing down time or do you accept the destructive consequences of your driving choices?. .❦. . Are you willing to learn self-love and with it, to slow down your time reality to feel what you love?

Breathe . . . slow down . . . your life moves as fast as you create it to move. By slowing down, you free yourself from the hyper-compression of time and provide the opportunity to enjoy life more.

Pearl Sixty-Nine

A Little at a Time

How often have you had tasks that you didn't want to do? As you procrastinate, it intensifies until it takes on all the characteristics of an impossible task. The avoidance cycle creates a situation infused with resistance. This type of resistance is a reflection of some part of you that is afraid to move forward in your life.

Our minds will attempt to force and demand that we address that fear to mobilize us. It may take years to build up enough explosive energy inside us to address our impacted resistance. Once we do, we may have enough passion to begin addressing the "mess." However, the pileup of chaos created by our persistent and consistent refusal to change and move forward may be so great that we cannot generate enough force to complete undoing the mess.

The consequence of this may create the following. We finally select a day committed to deal with the pile. Hours later, all the items from the messy closet are laid out chaotically all over the room. Suddenly, we can't stand the feeling of our piled up resistance, so we bolt, leaving the closet items spread everywhere in disarray. We're out of there. Days and days go by with the room in complete disarray. One day, in desperation since we can't stand the mess any longer, we gather up the items and stuff them back in the closet in worse shape than when we began.

When we do this, we know instinctively that our resistance and chaos have won once more. We sense we are victims of something inside ourselves that keeps us addicted to that agonizing pain that refuses to allow us to feel good about ourselves and our abilities to create what we love in our physical world.

I have a solution that works well for me and my students. I undo the mess the same way I created it, a little at a time. Instead of demanding that I undo a situation that has years of resistance locking it in place, I choose to do a little every day. That way, I don't have to face months or years of locked up resistance that the messy garage, closet, taxes, cabinets, filing cabinet, or whatever represents inside me. These items get messy because of chaos and refusal to live true to our hearts. To tackle this large a pileup in one day is usually exhausting and seldom successful.

Without living true to our hearts, we create patterns of forcing, resisting, and demanding in our physical world that resemble an overstuffed closet without a flow that is appropriate to the present time. Feel this out. Look in your house or office where the pileups are. This is truly a picture of the pileup inside yourself that is due to forcing, resisting, and demanding and has *nothing to do with loving yourself.*

Where the pileups exist, there is no appropriate flow of items. Often, one cannot access or find a necessary item in these piles of resistance even if desired. When these exist in your physical world, they also exist in your mind, body, and emotions. Because these patterns are created through the lack of love, they create pain due to blockage and limitation whether you are aware of it or not. See if you can get in touch with the pain of piles of resistance in your life.

If you designate a certain number of minutes a day—five to thirty minutes for example—in which you address the situation or a certain number of items that you move or throw away, you will be amazed at how easily and effortlessly you move forward. As you are doing this, you are literally peeling the chaotic inner onion one day at a time, the same way you created it. The exciting part of this is that as you address this one day at a time, you create new patterns that are more loving. By doing it in this way, you create a structure that helps you to keep the flow current in your home and office so that piles do not build up.

This is a process. If you persist, it will shift how you relate to your physical world. Eventually, you will move into more loving patterns in which your physical keeps up with your emotional and mental flows. This allows a balanced and non-chaotic flow. There is a deep sense of satisfaction and fulfillment when this occurs because this creates a natural connection to express your heart in your physical world.

As you adopt this type of patterning, you will find that it affects organization in every aspect of your life. Instead of creating pileups, you naturally move items to their proper place rather effortlessly. The exciting part of this is that it occurs with so little effort or focus. The organization naturally flows from your connection to what you love.

Are there areas of your life that are in tremendous disarray? . . ❦. . Each day, are you willing to heal a little of the chaos inside and physical pileup that created the problem? . . ❦. . Can you feel how many minutes a day you are willing to steadily apply to heal the pileup? . . ❦. . Do you love yourself enough to give this to yourself?

Self-love naturally creates orderly structures which create the most beneficial use and flow of your energy and time. Give yourself permission to free up the locked pockets of chaos and resistance that prevent this from occurring. You will love the freedom and sense of peace and balance that comes from this.

Pearl Seventy

Mind Illusions

I was absolutely convinced that my mind could solve and create a solution for any situation. When I look back on those old perceptions, I realize that my conviction was not based on any experiential data. I had blocked my emotional body and damaged my nearly closed heart, so that the only tool I still had functioning was my mind.

I lived much of my life in a default mode, where that part of me that was still operating was given recognition as the most important and valuable part. In this limited awareness, I wondered why those who demonstrated more heart-oriented realities didn't get a grip on their lives and stop wasting their energies on embarrassingly difficult emotions.

My mind patronized my own and others' hearts. I would tolerate them, but I was certain that my mind and theirs were all that really mattered. I felt that once they were more mature, they would abandon their feelings and hearts to focus on their minds.

I now feel that part of my ability to help others open their hearts is based on the experience of my own resistance to living in my heart. Looking back, I am shocked by how distorted my reality was.

As I began the process of opening my heart, I was consistently shown that if I released the rigid beliefs of my mind, my heart would step in and assist me in creating magic. It was through my creativity that I learned this. I had known all my life that I was supposed to be extremely creative. What came out, however, tended to be a short-lived trickle. My body moved rigidly, like an automaton with limited range. Generally, I avoided anything that involved being creative. I panicked if it was asked of me.

About fifteen years ago, a friend invited me to do extemporaneous acting in front of a video camera. My normal response would have been an adamant refusal. However, at that point in my life, I was a volcano ready for eruption.

Instead of refusing, I walked into a new reality dressed in an outrageous lavender polyester dress and an ugly wig. In front of the camera, a deeply suppressed comedienne burst through the rigid bonds that had shackled my heart and creativity. I amazed myself, as well as my friends. Humor effortlessly flowed from me without a script. The flow of creativity was so powerful that I felt I could have stayed in that flow for days without exhaustion or loss of humor. I had as much fun doing it as my audience did experiencing it. I was never the same!

My body started flowing. I exchanged the automaton reality for an exciting, three-year binge of creative play in which my many characters were expressed—often to the exclusion of my previous personality. I loved this time. Suddenly, my mind's rigidity was transformed into unending creativity, and my emotional body expressed the richness of my characters.

I learned then that my love and heart fueled my creativity. As I wrote screenplays and created opportunities for my characters to express my humor, I learned that mental rigidity was painful, limiting, and unbearably boring. I experienced the emotional richness of each of my characters.

Regrettably, my more established personality did not feel safe enough to access my own dynamic emotions. I was still willing to cry only for my characters, not myself. Sometimes, I see this pattern in my beginning students, who are willing to feel emotions for others, but rigidly refuse to feel their own.

The creative play ended as I felt my inner wisdom suggesting that I internally integrate all that I had learned and experienced through my beloved characters. At that point, I began unlocking my own emotions. I experienced how rich and important my feelings were and how limiting my mind had been. It was this lesson that gave me the courage and focus to learn to heal my heart and emotions and to assist others in doing the same.

Are you mentally locked into a rigid mental perception of reality that leaves little space for the warmth and dynamics of an aware feeling and heart nature? . .🌹. . Is your choice to deny your heart and feelings based on fear, severely limiting you and the creation and experience of your life? . .🌹. . Are you willing to awaken your feelings and heart to experience life from a much richer vantage point than you may be living at the present?

If so, self-love is an amazing doorway. Learning to feel and value your feelings, may unlock your creativity in a delightful and fulfilling way. For a rich life, this is definitely not to be missed.

Pearl Seventy-One

Doing, Doing, Doing!

In a world in which doing has the greatest perceived value—doing, doing, doing can be seductive. Unfortunately, if you overdo doing, your body and heart get tired and eventually want to die.

Life has much potential to be greater than the physical expression of action. Often, people overdo "doing" to run away from the pain of feeling. When this occurs, it is akin to blocking yourself from unlimited access to unlimited fuel that is created by the balance of action and non-action.

When you overdo, this forces your life out of balance. This lack of balance disconnects you from your unlimited source of fuel. Once this occurs, all the fuel that is left comes from the remaining "tank of gas" that is held in the cells of your physical body. Eventually, your body, like your car, will sputter to the side of the road, leaving you with depleted organs that have little life left. When this occurs, your options in life are gravely diminished. I have encountered many individuals who experienced this deep, stress-related cellular burnout.

You body is designed to refuel itself every day. It is through an open and expansive heart that the rest and recharging process occurs. Rest, pleasure, and joy provide your heart with the opportunity to refurbish and energize your body.

My experience with students is that the more convinced they are that they can't stop doing, the closer their bodies are to depletion. There is an enormous difference in refueling a body running on low versus empty.

This entire issue is about love. If you love yourself, you will create a life that feeds your body and feels good. If you don't, your mind will convince you that you must continue pushing and pushing, which depletes your body. If you start feeding love into your body and heart, everything will change. The stress-related diseases that threaten life are neutralized as your heart delights in creating a life that feels good.

One of my first students talked about his boss being a piranha who would call him in daily to chew him out. He kept doing, doing, doing to try to please his boss, and the results simply did not work. He was in pain, stressed out, and dreaded each day. It was affecting his health and life.

He worked at a major company that you would immediately recognize. Within the first nine months of study, he learned about self-love, how it felt, and how to create it. He reported that he and a group of co-workers gathered in the morning to plan their schedule, hugged each other warmly, and connected in their hearts before beginning the day as a result of his study of self-love. Each of the men looked forward to this warm exchange, even though it was at a major American corporation.

This student also reported that his boss had changed. This formerly despicable man began calling him into his office to discuss love and how it worked. He switched from attacks to meetings about love. Had you told the student before he began self-love studies that this would occur, he would have told you that you had no understanding of the business world or the people who were around him. He amazed himself with the power of his self-love.

Is your life in balance? . .🌹. . Do you create lavish time to meet your personal needs, or is your life stressed to the maximum? . .🌹. . Are you open to explore the possibility that if you learn to love yourself, everything in your world will transform to support you with love? . .🌹. . What are you waiting for?

As you get your life back in balance through love, perhaps your present world will start working to bless rather than destroy you. Doing, doing, and doing is seldom the answer. Loving yourself will unlock the doorway to greater love and ability to meet the needs of your heart and body.

Our Minds and Stress

Pearl Seventy-Two

Is Success Without the Heart Really Success?

I did not feel loved as a child. I loved, but I did not know how to create receiving love except through my animals and plants. This pain debilitated me and caused unusual health challenges that baffled doctors. My frightened parents bought me a small dog that they believe helped me survive through my childhood. I felt safe enough with Bootsee that I allowed his generous love to help sustain me.

Since I was very intelligent but I did not feel loved, I was convinced I could use my mind to create a world to receive what my heart was aching for. Consequently, I started a cycle of achieving. I could see patterns and possibilities that my peers would miss, and once I saw them I was able to create them unless it dealt with experiencing love. My desperation also drove me to work much harder than anyone else to earn love.

That was a powerful and unbearably painful combination. I was convinced that success would make me lovable and loved. In truth, however, I was raised in an environment where success seemed to drive me farther and farther from the goal of love. By my senior year in high school, I was tremendously disillusioned about the success and achievement cycle, yet I had no idea of how to replace it to receive love.

Receiving love begins within each of us. If we cannot receive love from ourselves, we have little possibility of receiving it from others. With my students, I teach, "It's the physics. If you can't receive love from yourself, it throws the physics off. It makes it very difficult to receive love from others." As a child, I expended enormous effort that did not help me receive love at all. In fact, it probably made the situation worse. Again, it was the physics. I totally missed the self-love piece.

Had I known how to love myself, the nurturing and richness this would have provided would have allowed me far greater success with much less effort. My creative genius would have been empowered by love, goodness, and fulfillment. My body would have responded to the self-love and created health which would have empowered everything. All that I would have done would have been centered on my experiencing more love and fulfillment. If I had felt a goal or project was not supporting me to feel loved, I would have known to adjust the situation rather than push and shove myself with harsher demands.

I know there are many of you in the same loop. Our families and business world often breed this as the formula for success. In truth, individuals caught in this belief damage their bodies through stress-related depletion.

True fulfillment is associated with experiencing the fullness of the heart. Yet, in today's world, many link their fulfillment with completing one more goal without the heart, then raising the bar for the next bigger goal. This creates a deadly pattern that depletes your heart and soul, and devalues life. If you are one of these individuals, *STOP*! Without love, the goals will never fulfill you. With self-love, your achievements will be infused with love and will bring you true fulfillment. Learn and master self-love. With it, success is as natural and easy as breathing.

Are you willing to give up goals which are not heart-based? . . ❧ . . Are you open to exploring the possibility of living self-love as a fundamental goal? . . ❧ . . Are you willing to allow your life to progress to a rich fulfillment through self-love?

Any true goal for success will have self-love as its focus and intent. Yum! . . . When you really understand this, it will open the possibility that you can live everything your heart desires. If your actions are motivated by self-love, then your creations become opportunities for experiencing self-love. Self-love is warm, always enough, stress-free, and abundant. The best will come from this.

Pearl Seventy-Three

Perfection Without the Heart Is Perfectly Painful

Because our society has lost focus on the value of the heart, it sets mental-based perfection as its highest value. Mental-based perfection is depleting, devaluing, and limiting. It keeps individuals focused on logic, critiques, and rules. In themselves, these are not bad aspects of our minds. The problem arises when the mental focus denies the value of the heart in the creative process.

When our minds strive for perfection without valuing our hearts, the following often occurs. The mind, usually through criticism, attacks the heart to keep it shut down. When this pattern exists, individuals are unable to bring the beautiful, fulfilling creativity of the heart into their endeavors. Without the heart having importance in our choices, we can blindly push ourselves to patterns and decisions that hurt, harm, and stress us.

The mind may firmly believe that the way to create success and a better life is to shut down the heart so that you can work long hours without rest, play, or nurturing. Without the heart to tell the mind that these attributes are equally important, the mind can eventually drive individuals into self-destruction, often diagnosed as a stress-related disease.

A healthy heart focuses on what feels loving and good in the present moment. If the heart is healthy and open, it is not fooled by tricks that our minds can and do play on us. If anything hurts or is harmful, the heart is *perfectly designed* to alert us. If each of us lived true to our hearts, then joy, abundance, and goodness would be richly experienced by all.

Shutting down our hearts' ability to tell us what feels good and blesses our physical lives leaves us vulnerable to patterns that can harm our bodies and make us want to die. So often, the feedback from our hearts is perceived as weakness and vulnerability, rather than being respected for the valuable protection that it provides. This wondrous fail-safe system is bypassed if our minds do not value, listen to, and respect our hearts.

In military training, one of the first lessons for recruits teaches them to devalue and ignore their hearts. As long as a recruit's heart is open, she or he is unable to push past harmful boundaries. In addition, an open heart cannot kill because killing another being, regardless of political orientation, is so painfully experienced by a heart-aware person. Every military organization knows that soldiers with open hearts cannot fight wars.

In a similar manner, some of our business leaders reward and value employees who display behavior associated with a closed, uncaring heart that enables them to push themselves and their employees beyond healthy boundaries.

Our minds can be like computers. They tell us what is appropriate by using logical and analytical evaluations based on programs and patterns inherited from our families and learned in life. If our programs and patterns were based on valuing the heart, then our minds would dutifully provide the necessary support to keep our hearts healthy and fulfilled. Unfortunately, few of us carry such patterns and programs. We may have some patterns that are supportive, but we likely have many others that are harmful to our hearts.

If you are truly seeking perfection in any area of your life, you must train your mind to support your heart in creating this perfection. Otherwise, your mind can push and distort your creation, causing you to harm your body through stress and to damage your heart's ability to support true perfection. *True perfection always has the goal of experiencing greater love as its focus.*

This does not mean you cannot have success as a goal. Self-love is tremendously creative, successful, and abundant. It means that in seeking to fulfill your goals, you must create a life that feels good and is deeply blessed with a loving and valued heart. When you do, your goals express themselves with fullness rather than depletion. Creations that are powered and supported by a loving heart are usually bigger than anything created without your heart.

Are you focused on living perfection rigidly controlled by your mind?

. .🌹. . Are you willing to relax this demanding perfection for the expansiveness and beauty of heart perfection? . .🌹. . Do you understand that a major clue to whether or not perfection is mental or heart-based is that mental perfection hurts and causes you to feel badly about yourself, regardless of what you do or achieve?

Heart-based perfection feels delicious, warm, and patient and always causes you to love yourself more and more.

Pearl Seventy-Four

Tricking Myself to Believe Lies as Truth

Physiological studies show that unless a baby is touched and loved, it will die. It is not an option. There is a threshold level of denial of love that makes sustaining life not possible. Babies and young children know and sense this at birth.

In dysfunctional families, such as homes of alcoholic or abusive parents where love is denied or not available, babies and young children operate dangerously close to this terrifying threshold. This activates a desperate survival mechanism within them.

They know they must have a certain level of love, caring, and touch to survive, but they aren't getting it. The human mind, seeking to help the child survive, begins playing tricks and creating illusions.

The dysfunctional and love-denying patterns of the parents are misidentified as love. The child knows it cannot survive without love, and this illusion is essential. The child's mind says, "I know you are desperate. The best I can do is reprogram you so that you identify that which isn't love as love. Then, you can trick yourself into believing that you have enough love to survive, even though you don't." This survival program actually helps in a desperate situation and enables these love-starved children to survive into their teenage years.

Unfortunately, the price for this is very, very high. Once the mind has tricked itself into believing abusive or love-denying patterns are love, then one has sealed his or her fate to attract others who will abuse him or her and deny love, as did his or her parents.

Imagine going to a movie and every time the character does something horrid to another character, you say to yourself, "This is love. That person really loves no matter what it looks like." It would confuse you. If you remained focused on this, eventually you would believe that abusiveness represented the word and concept of love. Because this was created by the survival fears of a desperate child, you would believe that you would die if you did not create this form of distorted, self-denying love. Yet, because of the misprogramming, your body would respond that you could not do without this illusionary love, which is actually lack of love.

Remember, the child was struggling at the threshold of not having enough love to physically survive. The child felt that unless he deluded himself, his body would die. This entire pattern is based on self-deceit.

While this makes it difficult enough to create appropriate patterns of love, the individuals that were not loved as children also lack a reference or blueprint for how true, supportive love feels. They desperately know that love is necessary to live. Yet, when it comes to creating love, they have been living under this illusion for so long that they literally cannot see clearly. Their bodies falsely tell them that love is actually the denial of love. They fear they will die if they face the truth—that their parents did not know how or were unavailable to love them.

They cannot sense or create true love because they can't relate to something they have not experienced. They must create new definitions of love that hold warmth, safety, and availability. Each of these healthy patterns of love can be created by them when they learn to relate to themselves with self-love. Once an individual lavishes enough self-love to reliably provide these patterns in his or her daily life, she or he can create an accurate reference that provides the opportunity for healthy relationships.

The good news is that since these desperate children misprogrammed their minds and bodies, they can reverse the process and program their minds to accurately identify and attract true love as adults. To do this, honesty in terms of what they see and feel must be deeply explored in order to find their childhood patterns about what love is and what love isn't. To heal this requires tremendous dedication and courage. Yet, all the good things that an individual can experience can only be found by unveiling the illusions and seeing truth accurately. It is from this place that warmth and supportive love is created.

Are you honest with yourself about others? . . ❦ . . Do you desperately keep veils of illusion and dishonesty about the quality of relationships you create? . . ❦ . . If not, are you willing to begin healing trickery about love?

In order to experience true love rather than illusionary love, you require an inner structure that appropriately feels, identifies, and responds to true patterns of love. To create this accurate physical, emotional, and mental structure, you must be willing to face the illusions you used to survive. This is an important doorway back to living true love.

Pearl Seventy-Five

To Whom Am I Mouthing Off?

My human mind fascinates me. When I would be alone, I would suddenly mouth off to someone, somewhere. I usually did it silently, but if I was upset, it might be out loud. I seldom had prior warning before I mouthed off. One moment, my mind was focused on my daily routine, and the next moment I was mouthing off, dissatisfied, and venting about how upset I was.

I would urgently demand that, "You had better take care of this or that," yet I had little faith that it would be appropriately addressed. Or I would lament, "This isn't fair. I am fed up, and you better do this, or I am going to quit, give up, or whatever." The mouthing off always had the essence of victimization. There was also a desperate belief that nothing was going to be done, and the victimization would continue forever.

This was not the vocabulary I used with myself or anyone else. It was only when I was tossing my disgruntled thoughts to someone in the great unknown that I would create this victimized language. One day, it occurred to me that I did not know to whom I was complaining. That seemed strange and, at the same, quite funny to me.

As a result, I began a mini-research project to learn what was really happening inside me when I was mouthing off. Although I am very spiritual, and prayer and communication with God is an important part of my life, I did not think God was my intended audience. If so, I was rather harsh and apparently expected little relief from God. This had none of the great love of God that is an essence of who I am. I was intrigued to get to the bottom of this mystery.

I decided that every time the desire to mouth off came, I would ask myself to whom I was talking before I continued my tirade. I would ask if I was speaking to God, my neighbor, or the great unknown, for example. With whom did I feel that the language of a victim was useful and appropriate?

The intended listener was not important as I became aware of the different places I directed my tirades. Amazingly, after I did this for a few days, I simply released the desire to mouth off. By choosing to stop and become aware of where I desired to communicate my perceived victimization, the desire to victimize myself in this way ceased. As I let go of this desire, my sense of security, empowerment, and general well-being increased.

Do you mouth off, venting victimized language at someone you know or don't know? . . ❧. . Are you ready to go beyond this disempowerment pattern? . . ❧. . Are you aware to whom you are communicating your mouthing off, or do you send it off into the unknown? . . ❧. . Are you willing to ask yourself where you are sending this venting in order to heal this part of you?

Any time we speak as a helpless victim, we are identifying parts of ourselves that are leaking part of our life force into the hopeless, helpless, and fearful. We choose when or if we heal this waste of our potential as love. Perhaps my mind was unique in having this mouthing off pattern. I included this pearl of wisdom in case I'm not the only one.

Pearl Seventy-Six

This Isn't Okay

How many times have you objected to something that wasn't okay in your life? Perhaps it is harsh or in some way prohibits you from living what your heart knows you deserve and desire. When this occurs for me, the words "this isn't okay" come to me.

Big Clue! When you say this to yourself or others, it indicates that you have a restriction that won't allow God's light into your heart. In other words, the light of God that helps us to create what we love is blocked or restricted. The effect in our physical world is not okay with us. Fortunately, we can free ourselves and move forward in creating what we love.

When we create restrictions to God's abundant and supportive light and love, we are not victims, even though we may feel that we are. We may have unknowingly created restrictions through fear or inherited restrictive physical, emotional, or mental patterns that create separation from God's love. The following suggestion can help free our bodies, minds, and feelings from these types of restrictions.

Suggestion: When something in your life isn't working and causes you to say that "it isn't okay" repeat the following at least three times.

I remove any holds, restrictions, agreements, or contracts that interfere with God's light coming fully into my heart and body.

If you are sensitive and very aware of your body, you may feel a shift or a tingle that lets you know you are moving these restrictions.

As you clear the runway to allow God's light to more easily come into your body, you reduce the likelihood of creating the same pain or hurt again. God's light can only bless you and your world to the extent you allow it. It is always our choice that determines how much of God's light we allow into our bodies and our world.

Are you willing to develop new agreements and/or contracts with yourself, God, and the Earth on how you live and learn lessons on Earth? . . ❦ . . Are you willing to create your inner agreements and contracts to be those that move you rapidly and clearly into experiences of an open, secure heart?

Giving God permission to fully enter our hearts and bodies so that we get to live, feel, and create what we love is a choice that is available to each of us. We give the command to transform into this delicious expression of ourselves. Or we can continue living as if we are a victim with all the accompanying discomforts as long as we choose. It is our life and, therefore, our choice.

Rebellion, Arrogance, and Intolerance

Pearl Seventy-Seven

Does Rebellion Really Serve Me?

Most of us believe that unless we rebel, we will lose our identity. What this really means is that we fear expressing and creating exactly what we love in our daily lives. Typically, this insecurity is accompanied by poor communication skills and confusion about appropriate boundaries.

We believe that rebellion can help us to create an identity that is free from others' control and influence. Alas, this is a trick to prevent us from creating as beings of love. Rebellion pushes away love, limits our creative power, and isolates us in patterns that prevent us from connecting and feeling that we are a valuable part of the whole. Rebellion always hurts!

During the terrible two's and teens, we associate rebellion with power. With enough rebellion, we think that we have power over our parents and authority figures. We don't understand that rebellion pushes and repulses everything.

If we use rebellion to create our own reality, we push our reality to a new opposite extreme. As long as we remain loyal to our rebellion, we have sacrificed our freedom to fully express who we are as beings of love.

Let's say we rebel from being like our parents. Rebellion locks us into a structure that opposes our parents. If it is not opposite, then it is not an option in our reality. The repulsion or pushing away through rebellion causes us to create tremendous pain because our rebellion forces us to run away, rather than simply to relax and allow our expression as beings of love. Our rebellion sets up our parents as the enemy, locks us into a war that has no victory, and tremendously limits our options.

As we mature and learn that we are creating every aspect of our reality, we discover a shocking truth. If we create every nuance of our reality, our rebellion can only rebel at that which we desire to create! We, in truth, are rebelling against ourselves.

When we create, our rebellion stands like an abusive guard repulsing our desire. This repulsive force creates either nothing, something less than, or the opposite of what our hearts are desiring. The physics of rebellion interferes with our creativity. And it leaves us isolated and unable to materialize what we love. Ouch!

Rebellion can be insidious, subconscious, and disappointing as it pushes away the very creation we desire to live. It seduces us away from our true power, which is based on love and unity. Rebellion tends to create instability, inability to commit, and resistance that bogs, slows down, or prevents success. It causes us to separate from love, connection, and God, which can make us feel as though we don't belong or fit in. Pain always comes from this.

Once we heal our rebellion, it is amazing how much richness and peace enters our lives. We can create without interference to our creation. Healing rebellion has everything to do with awakening our creative genius. Feel it out.

Are you open to experiencing more connection with others and God? . . 🌹 . . Do you value your or your children's rebellion? . . 🌹 . . Does rebellion create a false sense of security for you? . . 🌹 . . If you release the resistance of rebellion, how would that free your heart to create what it loves?

Your connection to God is at stake when you are rebellious. As long as you value your rebellion, you are saying that you are not quite ready yet for your full potential of love, connection, and God.

Pearl Seventy-Eight

Rebelling Against What I Love

Part of my expertise is helping my students to heal their rebellion patterns. After her first intensive, a sixteen-year-old told me that she was very frightened. Even though she passionately wanted to complete her spiritual studies, she related, "I'm scared that I will use my rebellion to turn me away from my path. I'm rebellious, and I'm around rebellious people. I'm scared I won't make it through my studies because of my rebellion." I had been a mentor to this beautiful, highly intelligent young lady for several years and dearly loved her. It would take self-mastery on her part not to use her sharp mind to hurt her heart.

I explained that I had been developing new ways to help people out of the pain of rebellion and asked if she desired to do some research with me. She was excited and agreed. When she arrived at my home, I had her relax. Then, I asked her to remember a situation in which rebellion threatened her ability to create what she loved. Instantly, her body tensed.

I told her to say the following as she accepted her rebellion as completely as possible. "I lovingly accept my rebellion that causes me to fight with my parents." Immediately, she panicked. She thought that by accepting her rebellion, she would remain rebellious forever.

I stopped her and said, "That is what holds rebellion in place. Rebellious people cannot *lovingly accept anything*. That's the way rebellion works. If you accept it, it will move through your body, and that will be the end of that particular stream of rebellion." She looked at me with fear, then she remembered that she trusted me. So we tried again, letting her feel the rebellion that was keeping her in conflict with her parents.

Suddenly, she relaxed enough that as she repeated the words I gave her, the rebellion dissolved. Her body shuddered and her feet pushed down as an uncomfortable feeling traveled through her body. I explained that the strange, yucky feeling that she experienced was caused by the rebellion.

"Releasing rebellion is a little bit like an electrical surge that causes the phone to make strange static sounds," I explained. "Removing the static may feel uncomfortable, but it alerts you that a big charge of rebellion inside you is being discharged. Once the charge moves through your body, it is out of the way and no longer hurts you. Your body may not have a tangible response when rebellion uplifts, but sometimes it does."

As my student repeated her affirmation and accepted her rebellion, she moved through many, many issues in her life. I continued helping her until I was confident that she knew how to do this on her own and trusted this way of dealing with her rebellion.

When I saw her a month later, I asked her how our research project was going. She reported that it had changed her life. She wasn't fighting with her parents any more, and her rebellious friends were disappearing from her life. Love started entering her life from all directions once she began the process of healing.

I highly recommend this affirmation for those who are ready to heal their rebellion. The results are quite profound. Fill in the blank below on the nature of the rebellion, e.g. refuse to keep a clean home, push love away, fight people I love, etc.

Affirmation: *I lovingly accept my rebellion that causes me to_____.*

Do you trust yourself to walk out of your rebellion? . . . . Are you willing to take responsibility for this healing? . . . . Do you have enough self-love to support yourself in freeing your rebellion?

You are truly the master of your reality. You make the call on if you are a loving or an abusive master to yourself. Healing your rebellion moves you forward into being a loving master of your life.

Pearl Seventy-Nine

Freeing My Rebellious Mind

My Florida driver's license was scheduled to expire on my birthday. Since I was moving to North Carolina, my plan was to get my driver's license when I arrived in town. When I went to the Motor Vehicle Department to exchange my Florida license for a North Carolina one, I was shocked to be handed a written test.

I took the test cold because it was close to quitting time, and my license was scheduled to expire the next day. When I learned that I had missed more than I had gotten correct, I lovingly asked, "Did I pass?" I had been so successful with self-love pulling me out of potential holes so many times before that it would not have surprised me if the officer had responded with some loving loophole. However, I cringed a bit when he said, "You're kidding! With a score like that?"

But the next day was my birthday. Traditionally, I do only that which pleases my heart on my birthday. For this birthday, I awoke to the harsh reality that I had to study. While there were many things that I would have loved to learn, the driving rules of North Carolina were very low on that list.

Holding true to self-love principles as much as I could, I started to read the North Carolina driving manual, but I quickly realized that my rebellious mind had no intention of studying on my birthday. For hours, I stayed there, but my comprehension was basically nil.

It was my birthday, and I had created a situation that was forcing me to do what I did not want to do. It became obvious to me the next year was about mastering my rebellious mind. God had decided to start me off on this major project the first day of my birthday year.

I evaluated my choices. One was to continue rebelling against North Carolina's driving rules and waste—oops, spend—the rest of my birthday attempting to remember enough to pass. Another option, which didn't feel acceptable at all was to drive without a current driver's license. Immediately rushing back to Florida to renew my license felt too hard. Besides, I still had business in North Carolina. My last option was to deal with my rebellious mind. I chose to face that one.

By giving up my desire to rebel and push away, I was able to maintain focus on the driving book. I allowed my mind to pay attention and support my success to remember the necessary information. I focused with all my might until I could remember every word. The minute my rebellion would pop in and I lost focus, I would stop and deal with it. Then I would make the choice that I desired to remember the information more than I desired to rebel against it. As I did this I eventually cleared out enough rebellion so maintaining focus became easy.

Happily, I passed my North Carolina driver's license with an excellent score and still had some time to experience what my heart desired on my birthday.

For the entire next year, whenever I would feel my rebellion hurt me, I would do what I had to do to heal that part of me. As I did this, I could sense how much easier college would have been had I known how to deal with my rebellious mind. This experience convinced me that some learning disorders are probably caused by rebellion. As a result of this experience, I can now help my students heal their rebellion much faster than I could initially.

Do you recognize when you are in rebellion? . . .❧. . Are you a victim of your rebellion, or do you shift it when you sense it? . . .❧. . Are you willing to let your rebellion go or would you rather stay stuck in your own resistance?

Your focus and ability to remember is linked with being present. When you rebel against a concept, your mind will prevent you from comprehending or remembering it by pushing your focus away from it. This limits your options of using your mind to support creating what you love.

Pearl Eighty

Aching Pain in My Body

We live in a country where rebellion is thought to maintain power and express one's uniqueness. Unfortunately, we pay a very high price for rebellion. We push from one uncomfortable extreme to another.

The price of rebellion is often pain in our bodies. Very uncomfortable, creepy feelings are associated with rebellion. It makes us feel that we can't tolerate or handle something or someone. These feelings are so unpleasant that we try to avoid awareness of the rebellion. This avoidance creates numbness that helps lock rebellion into our bodies and lives. Deep, deep pain is created because rebellion separates us from our natural ability to love and express ourselves as loving, empowered creators.

This intense discomfort leads us to deny rebellion exists, and to hide it in our subconscious. This causes pain in our bodies and feelings of panic associated with not being able to stand being in our body. Rebellion can be so painful that we find life too overwhelming and question if it is worth living.

Too much rebellion can cause disease because it pushes away energies that are necessary to sustain a healthy body. I believe rebellion can cause the cells in your body to push and oppose each other which interferes with the natural flow and cellular communication that is necessary for healthy body chemistry. Your cells work against each other rather than create a harmonious, peaceful body.

If your pain is caused by rebellion, this affirmation will help you to clear it rather quickly, and your life will generally work better. Also, if you feel tense or restless, say this affirmation until your feelings improve. This will free you from the bondage of rebellion. You will be amazed at the ease and shift you experience.

Affirmation: *Rebellion has no time, space, or authority in our world.*

Are undiagnosed feelings of pain in your body normal for you? . . ✤. . Do you hear yourself thinking: "I can't stand it," or "I feel like going crazy"? . . ✤. . Do you question if life is worth the effort? . . ✤. . Are you interested in freeing yourself of this type of discomfort?

As you heal your vulnerability to rebellion, chances are the next day at work may not be so difficult. You may notice that the neck aches and unexplained pains diminish. As a bonus, you may be able to create something on the physical that has been stuck and in resistance for a while.

Pearl Eighty-One

Intolerance

When I first began my spiritual journey, I was told that my many lessons would include learning and teaching about how to heal intolerance. A wise counselor explained that my mind would experience intolerance, and this would create grave suffering for my heart. She cautioned that as long as I was intolerant of other's intolerance, even if it was directed towards me, I was still intolerant. I would not be free of intolerance until my mind no longer created it in any form.

To heal this part of me, I would respond to my intolerance for someone or some situation by saying, "Sweetie, what are you intolerant of inside yourself? This person for whom you feel intolerance is showing you where you are intolerant of yourself. I love you. What about me are you intolerant of?" As I worked with this, my intolerance dissolved leaving me free to express my great love for others.

One of my students was struggling with this pattern. He frequently experienced intolerance, immediately felt a harsh judgment against a person, and then directed it towards himself for his being judgmental. He would run away from the person in a futile attempt to escape his intolerance and harsh judgment, isolating himself in loneliness, which hurt his heart.

I worked with him to heal this pattern. Whenever he felt his intolerance, he would blink his eyes and silently say, "No judgment." He loved this technique, which allowed him to no longer be a victim of his intolerance. As he worked with this, his intolerance dissolved.

There is another type of intolerance that creates prejudice. This type of intolerance tends to be passed from one generation to another. The core of disruption that creates prejudice, I believe, is rebellion. In order for prejudice to heal, one must first desire that it heal. Family and social structure tends to perpetuate the illusion that prejudice is valuable and appropriate. In truth, it harms everyone.

If you struggle with prejudice, I suggest that you first get clear if you are motivated to heal this part of yourself. Then, I would advise reciting this affirmation every day and whenever you experience the feelings of prejudice.

Affirmation: *Rebellion and intolerance have no time, space, or authority in our world.*

Is intolerance a discomfort you experience? . . ❧ . . If so, what forms does it take for you? . . ❧ . . Are you willing to free yourself of it?

If you experience intolerance or prejudice, the one you are actually intolerant toward is yourself. Giving up your intolerance and prejudice frees you up to allow your heart to express its true ability to love. What a marvelous reward for this peace within yourself.

Pearl Eighty-Two

Plain Old Garden-Variety Arrogance

Every organization probably has one or two arrogant individuals that drive people from them. You may even be one of them. But if it's inside you, arrogance feels impossible to escape, no matter how uncomfortable – because if you are arrogant, it goes where you go.

Whether you have arrogance around you or you are caught in its grip, soften up! I would like to burst the illusion—the bubble of untruth—about arrogance. Arrogant people are not terrible people despite their efforts to convince everyone otherwise. In truth, they are extremely insecure and feel very unloved and unvalued. They need love, approval, and compassion which ultimately must come from within them. I can hear you retort, "Oh, no, they're not. They are obnoxious beings who think they know everything." In reality, they try to cover up their insecurity by pretending they have it together and are all-knowing.

So here is the story about arrogance. If you are arrogant and push people around with it, start loving yourself. Love yourself as you would a hurting child who feels unloved, unvalued, and insecure. Whenever you catch yourself being overbearing to others, soften up as you say,

"I love myself unconditionally. I give myself extra love when I am arrogant because I am feeling insecure."

If someone else is making your life unbearable because of his or her arrogance, realize he or she is hurting and insecure. Say the following:

Affirmation: *I especially love myself and others unconditionally when we are arrogant.*

Watch what happens to the situation with that person. You may be amazed. Because we are all mirrors to each other, you will not be troubled by their arrogance unless you are in pain about your own. If you are not judging your arrogance, chances are it will be easy to be accepting about theirs!

Do you feel you are a terrible person if you face the fact that you may be arrogant? . .🌹. . Does your love encompass arrogance in yourself and others? . .🌹. . Are you willing to heal arrogance by addressing your insecurities?

Deep acceptance is a powerful way to free ourselves of painful insecurities and imperfections. It requires self-love to create self-acceptance. As you develop this for yourself, unconditional love becomes a natural way of relating to others.

Pearl Eighty-Three

Inner Peace

Americans, along with the rest of the world, have been challenged to find a deeper level of peace within themselves in the midst of shocking terrorism, that may cause us to believe we may never feel truly safe again. Ultimately, the victory over wanton destructiveness must be won within the hearts of each of us.

Until we find inner peace in the midst of events that can feed a belief that fear is real and justified, we give a violent, crazy group of individuals the power to disrupt the harmony that is our birthright. It is the inner peace within the heart of every child and adult that will collectively choose how much we suffer or how much we transcend beyond the vulnerability to become fearful.

Fear can have a tremendous grip on our emotions, creativity, and bodies. When it does, it debilitates and limits our options, which sets us up to experience more of what we fear.

Years ago, I had a friend who was terrified of pit bulldogs. The only time I have ever been aware of seeing a pit bulldog was when I was with this friend. Without exception, she would see these animals every time we went anywhere. Her obsessive fear literally created them everywhere she was.

Many years ago, I had a similar obsessive fear about snakes. Once, a snake fell on my body as I walked out of my porch door and set in motion a cascade of fear experiences with snakes. Over a year-and-a-half period, I had about ten snakes appear in my home. Some were sunning in my den;

others I almost stepped on. One was curled up in my down sofa, and on and on. I went from a place of never thinking about snakes to being obsessively afraid to step without fear that another snake would be there. It was truly a horrible way to live.

My obsessive fear of snakes, supported by more and more experiences to validate my fear, went everywhere I went, both inside and outside my home. There was no inner peace because I had chosen to give my fear of snakes power over me. The more I gave away my inner peace, the more validation I created in my physical experiences to say that snakes were everywhere to scare and hurt me.

Finally, as an act of mercy, I woke up one morning and said to myself, "I can't live with the fear of snakes anymore. No snake could be worse than my fear." With this inner clarity, I spoke with God and made the following agreement, "God, for the rest of this lifetime, if there is a snake near me, I will sense it in plenty of time to create a relaxed and natural feeling of safety for myself and those I love. I am exchanging my fear of snakes for this agreement between you and me."

For the past fifteen years, that has been consistently what has occurred for me. I can feel them if they are near and am very relaxed about it. I know that my safety from harm or even experiences that would scare me is consistently assured by my love of God. I am deeply at peace with snakes and any tendency to fear them.

So I would like to share with you how I am dealing with the potential of more terrorism in our country. My heart is very clear with God that I do not choose to participate in violence in our country whether as a victim of it or through using my inner fears to help create more to fear. Also, I am equally clear that I also am choosing to support those beings whom I love to be free of any vulnerability to wanton violence.

My heart has chosen to free itself of fear for myself, for those I love, and for that which I love. My focus is to create a reality through my inner peace that validates freedom from fear.

Are you willing to free yourself from fear that feeds violence and terrorism? . . . Are you willing to create safety for yourself and show your love through your connection to God? . . . Are you willing to create a deeper inner peace that is not dependent on external validation?

Inner peace is a powerful creative force that exists within the heart of those who desire peace over fighting and war. This deep inner peace is a choice.

Bridge Between My
Mind and Heart

Pearl Eighty-Four

Creating a Loving Bridge
Between My Mind and Heart

A lot of God's love and light enters through the top of our heads. That is why if you asked where heaven or where God is, people tend to point up. If God's love and light remain predominantly in our minds or heads, we tend to be very mental and focused in our thoughts. If, however, we bless ourselves by allowing God's love and light to flow into our hearts, not only do we have the benefit of our minds, we also experience the richness of feeling God in our hearts. Most of my teachings focus on learning to allow God's love and light into our hearts.

A wonderful scientist named Björne W. Nordenström[2] conducted thorough research to demonstrate that the circulatory system in our bodies is very much like the electrical circuits found in your stereo or computer. These biological circuits are crucial in terms of healing and creating healthy bodies.

In order for individuals to bring God's light from the top of their heads into their hearts, the necessary internal electrical circuits must exist to transfer the electromagnetic energy into their hearts. I call this the electrical bridge between our minds and hearts. Individuals who have a healthy connection between their minds and hearts have a natural energetic flow that feeds the heart and brings awareness of joy and wholeness. The beauty and pleasure that comes from this love is truly worthy of pursuit.

Unfortunately, some of the physical, emotional, and mental patterns we inherit and learn can create trauma that damages or sometimes literally severs this electrical bridge between our minds and hearts. By numbing my emotions, I lived this way for many painful years.

Likewise, the electrical bridges of some of my students would short-circuit, rather than allowing their love and light to correctly feed and nurture their hearts. This short-circuit could make them appear to be defensive and aggressive when they are in situations that encourage them to experience their feelings and their hearts. Or, they might perceive themselves as fine even though they are numb to their feelings and heart nature, because they do not have a direct link between their minds and hearts. Not uncommon to individuals with long-term numbness, they may be depleted and experience severe health challenges as a result.

The key to reconnecting or restructuring the electrical bridge between the mind and heart is a *passionate desire to value and feel the heart.* Any belief denying the value of the heart or any fear about the nature of our minds interferes with the correct operation of this electrical bridge. I have found that it takes enormous passion to restructure a severely damaged or blocked electrical bridge to regain an open, free-flowing connection between the mind and heart. When individuals attempt to feel love or to open to healthier expressions of love, pain from the damaged or severed electrical bridge directs them to shut down their feelings even more or to deny the value of the mind-heart connection. This is a very painful trap.

Until an individual has enough passion and desire to feel his or her own ability to love, he or she tends to run away from patterns and opportunities that would support this healing. The damaged electrical bridge may short-circuit and be experienced as uncaring, no ability to feel one's heart, or electrically exploding, which is perceived as rage or hostility directed at the energies or situation seeking to restructure the electrical bridge.

That is why so much passion is required by the person valuing and desiring to return his or her heart to full awareness. He or she must remain true to passion for the heart as the body creates new pathways to restructure the electrical bridge. Uncomfortable physical pain may accompany this restructuring.

When the electrical bridge is correctly connected, the mind loves and protects the heart, and the heart opens and allows the mind's light to enter for support. This creates a closed electrical circuit that connects the mind and heart and allows them to function together to create well-being and good-ness. When this electrical circuit is closed and operating correctly, the individual feels a natural spiritual connection in the body called wholeness.

I have personally walked through this process. I now help others walk it more easily than I was able to do. I am so grateful that I had the courage to sustain the desire to heal and open my heart to reconnect this electrical bridge.

Feel. Is your electrical bridge between your mind and heart healthy and dynamically rich? . . ❦ . . Or is it so damaged or severed that you feel little or nothing in your heart? . . ❦ . . If that is the case, do you have enough passionate desire to heal your heart that you are willing to restructure this part of yourself?

Creating a structure between your mind and heart that supports whole-ness allows God to bless your life through love. This blessed connection is truly worthy of pursuit.

[2]Nordenström, Björn E. W., <u>Biological Closed Electric Circuits</u>, Almqvist & Wikell, Uppsala, Sweden, 1983.

Pearl Eighty-Five

Rejecting Love No More

I never plan my introductory classes. I feel the group and use my intuition to determine the most beneficial teaching for the students assembled. One night as I was teaching an introduction, I sensed that this group personified loneliness and abandonment from rejecting love, and I talked about this painful pattern. Only after the workshop began that next day did I understand the complexity of this pattern.

Each one of the us, for I was in this group also, was extremely sensitive as children. A misplaced look, a misunderstood word, or a harsh tone could readily cause pain and shock us. Although we were capable of creating severely painful life experiences, as many of us had, a raised eyebrow was sufficient to create perceived hurt, as well. Feeling we could not handle this world and the pain associated with it, we had learned to withdraw and pull into ourselves whenever we were hurt.

During the workshop, we discovered that this created a pattern of isolation that no one, not even those who loved us, could penetrate. If we held the isolation long enough, the people whom we loved would feel rejected and would usually leave. When this occurred, we would feel devastated, perceiving that the person we loved rejected and abandoned us.

Conversely, our withdrawal created the person that we loved to believe that we had rejected him or her. Because of this pattern, we were terrified of being abandoned. Our fear created enormous stress and undermined our relationships. We didn't realize how we created the abandonment and used our sensitivity to hurt ourselves.

We would also tend to believe that we were too hurt or too sensitive to communicate. So, when we were hurt, our withdrawal included withholding information from those we love. They seldom understood what had happened or how to prevent our next withdrawal.

As we saw how this pattern affected our lives, we explored how self-love could heal it. None of us realized that when we made the choice to withdraw within ourselves, we were rejecting love and creating our next abandonment. By the end of the day, everyone was extremely tired from seeing something within themselves that had been so painful. I sent everyone to their homes and hotels and told them to be very gentle with themselves and rest.

During the first day of that workshop, a beautiful woman revealed that she was so hurt by her divorce five years earlier that the only solace she felt was through her horses. She had moved into the barn and slept near them for several months after her divorce. At our next class, she was beaming from ear to ear and appeared happy and self-confident.

She reported that upon returning home, her fiancée unknowingly hurt her feelings as he greeted her. She quickly excused herself and went upstairs to withdraw into her hurt. Within moments she thought, "Stop. I know he loves me. If I love myself like I learned to love myself today, I can deal with this." So, she poured love inside her heart and soon felt that she was back in her center. She returned downstairs to share what had happened with him.

Unaware that he had hurt her, her fiancée apologized profusely. However, she stopped him, explaining, "I know you love me. I used my sensitivity to separate us. I don't want to do that any more." They hugged and had a wonderfully intimate evening. She told us that if she had not learned a new way to manage this pattern, it would have taken several weeks for the relationship to mend. With her new understanding of herself and the power of her self-love, it took less than five minutes.

Are you a victim of your own sensitivity? . . . Do you use your sensitivity to create isolation and the perception that you cannot handle living? . . . Are you open to learning new ways to deal with your sensitivity? . . . Do you realize that when you create separation, it will eventually result in rejection and abandonment?

We are not victims of our sensitivity, nor are we victims of abandonment and rejection—no matter how real this feels and appears. If you have this pattern, learn to recognize when you are rejecting love by withdrawing into isolation. Explore how to communicate your feelings without blame. You can learn to love yourself to support your sensitivity being a blessing rather than something that creates separation, pain, and abandonment.

Pearl Eighty-Six

When My Mind and Heart Love Each Other

Returning to that inner space where the mind and heart love each other can be extremely frightening. It is akin to a candy or toy shop that we are trained to avoid simply because it is too good. The ability to create internal, balanced love between your mind and heart may be barricaded with dire warnings on the doorway, such as the following:

> Danger, too much blessed power of love. Turn around and avoid.
> My body and emotions can't handle this.
> Avoid to prevent body overload of too much bliss and joy.
> This will eliminate my desire to fight myself and others.
> Can I be safe without war?
> Avoid this unknown territory.

Obviously, these warnings would discourage all but the most courageous. It is to those who persevere that I speak. Yes, when the mind and heart are correctly aligned to loving yourself in every cell of your body, there is a massive increase in power, joy, and bliss. This can bring forth a magnitude of love, success, and divinity that may now rest quietly as a memory of perfection within you. How do we get past our internal warnings that scare us away from loving ourselves so completely? . . . Self-love is the key.

Whenever you seek power for power's sake, you are in a potentially dangerous territory because you do not have the protection of an open heart. An open heart tells you what feels good, what is safe, and what protects your body in our world. However, you cannot merge the heart and mind unless you love yourself. Loving yourself protects you from those unproductive warnings and allows you safe passage into this land of the power of love, truth, and peace.

For the courageous individuals who seek to have their minds and hearts loving each other, I suggest the following exercise.

In front of a full-length mirror (at least two feet by five feet), relax your body by breathing deeply. Send a loving thought about yourself from your mind to your heart. Then, get very still and see if your heart will open to feel the loving thought. As your heart opens, notice how much your heart loves your mind. Also, notice how much your mind loves to support you in this way. As you develop skill with this exercise, your mind will easily form wonderful thoughts of love about you, and your heart will naturally open to receive these loving thoughts.

Through this exchange of love, you are literally creating circuits that connect your heart and mind which I previously referred to as the electrical bridge. This process is similar to creating a loving relationship with some-one you care about. It takes time to develop the trust and the connections, and it is worth it. This begins the process of your mind and heart learning to love each other.

After you have developed proficiency with your mind and heart loving each other and have completed the above exercise, do the following one.

Begin again by sending a loving thought about yourself. As you open your heart to receive your mind's loving thought, expand and open your entire body to receive it as well. Especially open your body from your heart down to your toes to receive the love of your mind.

This powerful exercise feels wondrous and will bring much goodness into your world and help heal the electrical bridge between your mind and heart.

Eliminating Fear, Victimization, and Frantic Feelings

Pearl Eighty-Seven

"Petrification"

One of my students was trying to relax enough to free the soft, intimate, and loving part of her heart. She said she felt like a terrified cat that was frozen into a locked position and clinging to the top of the tree. She simply was too afraid to do what her heart desired. She wanted to get down from the tree and participate in life in a loving way, yet her body was rigid and locked into a shock pattern.

As I helped her, I used the term "petrification" to describe her state of terror. I said it to help her break through her fear, and we both laughed. However, I feel this term captures the essence of the problem. When she was a child, she had life experiences that created a permanent state of immobilizing fear.

It reminded me of an incident with my sister. When she was very young, she plugged a bobby pin into an electrical outlet. The electrical shock violently blew her body away from the electrical connection and saved her life. Sometimes, a shock simply freezes the person's muscles, gluing and immobilizing him or her to the source of pain. That is what happens in petrification. Something so shocking and painful happens that a person's emotional self freezes. Only the terror exists. The petrification eliminates his or her options to choose something more beneficial. The horror of the experience shocks her or his delicate electrical system into a permanent frozen pattern.

Different healers have different approaches to working with pain patterns such as this. My preference is to use sweetness and self-love to dissolve it. As my student experienced petrification as a child, the thing she most desperately wanted to hear and feel was that someone she loved was there to assist and love her, and everything would be all right.

I teach people who have this type of terror to speak sweetly and patiently to themselves, to never push or be demanding, and to frequently ask the frightened part how they can help it to feel safer. I teach them to be lovingly present for themselves. The following are phrases that I use to help individuals build trust of themselves:

> What do I need, Sweetie?
> I'm right here for myself.
> How can I help this to be easier?
> I'm always here for myself.
> I love myself. I care.
> Everything is going to be all right.

Are you aware of any patterns of petrification in your body? . .❦. . Are you willing to soothe and comfort these painful memories to release them from your body, heart, and feelings? . .❦. . Are you willing to be very patient as you seek to release this type of frozen fear?

Once you feel that you are learning to love yourself and avoid pushing and demanding, the petrification tends to unlock. For some individuals, it is faster than for others. Either way, learning to dialogue with self in a way that builds trust is extremely valuable.

Pearl Eighty-Eight

But I Thought I Was the Good Guy

I remember when I first started healing my emotional body. I had created and lived patterns of victimization all of my life. I had a very self-righteous feeling that if I was the victim, I was the good guy, and the individual who victimized me was the bad guy.

I was certain that God loved me more as a victim than God loved the victimizer. I was very noble and self-righteously assured that by wearing the badge of a victim, I created the good guy image that would receive God's love.

As I examined my pent-up feelings and disruptive mental patterns, I was shocked at what I observed. I discovered that it consistently took the same amount of energy to heal being a victim as it did to heal being a victimizer. This was a tremendous affront to my noble, self-righteous, good-guy pattern. It stripped away my noble pursuit.

As I came to understand this pattern, I realized that God probably didn't have much preference whether someone refused to express his or her power of God's love as a victim or to harm others as a victimizer. In the end, it requires the same amount of effort to heal either one. This was life-changing for me.

As I learned the similarities of these patterns, I realized that both of them were controlling, dominating, and these both avoid the secure power of love as a way of life. A victim could not exist without a victimizer, and conversely, a victimizer could not exist without a victim.

I remember thinking, "But that's not fair. I'm the good guy. They're so bad and mean. God couldn't love them, because they're mean to the good guy." I was deeply invested in self-righteously supporting my noble role as a victim.

As I matured into the above understanding, it helped to free myself from judgment. I could feel that any desire on my part to convince God that being a victim was better than being a victimizer was not in harmony with God's true nature of love. This entire pattern was a trick of my mind to keep me attached to victimization, thereby debilitating my abilities, creativity, and love.

My heart came to realize that someday both the victim and victimizer will probably choose to abandon these patterns and return to the secure power of God's love.

Are you self-righteous about being a victim? . . 🌹 . . Can you feel how this helps you to stay invested in victimization patterns that hurt you? . . 🌹 . . Do you desire to remain a victim or are you ready to walk out of this pattern so you can live what you love?

Freeing oneself of the desire to be a victim is a necessary step to walk forward into living the true power of love.

Pearl Eighty-Nine

Going So Fast I Feel Crazy

My mind often raced so quickly that I would become frantic and feel as though I might go crazy. I hung out for years on that terrifying edge, uncertain whether I could maintain my sanity. Happily, I no longer experience this. For those of you that struggle with a frantic mind, I'll explain how I tamed mine.

First of all, this is not unusual for individuals with powerful minds and strong, creative abilities. Individuals who have insanity in their families may also have this tendency. I had to deal with both.

I believe that more than half the lineages with insanity are those in which the mind lost its ability to relate accurately to home and family. Without the warmth and stability of a loving family, the mind revolts and may race in an effort to escape the abuse and lack of love.

So, if your mind is racing, pay particular attention to your home. Whether you live by yourself or with others, place particular attention on creating a home you love. Your home will stabilize you and help you to handle a quick mind. Fluff pillows, drink warm tea, cook, decorate, putter in the yard, and spend quiet time with someone in your home to help yourself adjust to loving patterns associated with home and family. This brings balance into your mind and helps you to develop a more accurate view of reality.

When your mind is frantic and going faster than you can handle, try not to slow it down directly. When I have attempted this, it felt like throwing a monkey wrench into fast-moving gears. The resistance generated caused me to feel as though my brain was smoking and burning.

I learned to eliminate this problem by asking myself, "What are you feeling, Sweetie?" The instant I focused on my feelings, it was like unplugging a fan that was going too fast. Because I was not trying to force my mind to slow down, it slowed down at its own pace, minimizing the resistance, damage, and self-destructive responses.

I now can feel if my mind is racing, if words or thoughts come too fast for my peaceful comfort. If I feel this, which I seldom do anymore, I will lovingly say to myself, "Sweetie, too many words." When I say this, I take my focus to my feeling self and am no longer available to listen to an inner tirade of too many words.

If my mind was going too fast, I felt my emotions and lavished myself with as much slow, self-love for myself as possible. Soaking in water—which soothes and stimulates the feeling nature—was also helpful. Walking and talking more slowly than normal also slows everything down and helps the mind to relax.

In addition, I learned to never make a decision or try to accomplish anything when I was in a frantic state. Through much experience, I learned to recognize the internal illusions and tricks that said I had to have an immediate answer or had to complete something right away. I learned to respond, "I need time to feel this out to make the best choice."

When there was a deadline, I learned to convey my need for extra time to deliver a quality product. Once I stated this, I was always given the necessary time. I learned that it was my mind's driving panic and fear that compressed reality in the first place. Once I created enough inner peace by moving into awareness of my slower feeling nature, my physical reality gratefully supported a more balanced, peaceful, and slow reality. Invariably, the no-choice, have-to, desperate situation that was created by my racing, frantic mind would dissolve to support me having adequate time.

Through these lessons, I learned how fluid reality is. Reality immediately shifts when I am clear enough to express what I need. My world slows down when I truly desire it and am willing to dissolve the fear pushing my mind.

I love the release from this terrifying problem. By healing this part of me, I am able to create a safer, more secure world. In addition, I no longer experience the pain, burning sensations, and knotted up muscles I felt in my body when my mind was frantic. If I healed this, so can you!

The next time your mind goes too fast, try the following:

Walk and talk half as fast.

Ask, "What am I feeling, Sweetie? I'm here for me."

If you sense too many inner words, too fast, lovingly say, "Sweetie, too many words." Return focus to your feeling self.

Table any desire to figure out or make any decision until you are no longer frantic.

Trust that once you slow down, most of the "frantic demands" will collapse and become unimportant.

Comfort the fears that revved you up.

You will love gaining mastery over your racing mind. In its place comes peace and harmony that allows you to create a loving sense of security of being you.

Pearl Ninety

Whirlybirds

Have your mind and emotions ever been in such turmoil that you couldn't escape the cause of your distress? I call these whirlybirds. For example, someone hurts your feelings, and you can't let it go. You grind and grind remembering them and the situation, feeling hurt and victimized, the more you go around and around with the toxic thoughts and feelings. Through great effort on your part, in this churning about the person and hurt-laden situation, you create a mini-tornado ready to wreak havoc in your world.

As the spinning whirlybird feeds itself with blame, hatred, and rage at yourself, another person, or a situation, you unwittingly create yet another round of disruption that is guaranteed to create more stress for yourself. Your mind and emotions have synchronized in a coordinated effort to create something that will hurt you and perhaps someone else. Only with deep restoration of peace within will you be able to restore peace and heal the stress of the whirlybirds of negative thoughts and emotions.

These whirlybirds can be stopped before they transform into mini- or mega-tornadoes if they are detected in time and if you have enough self-love to desire harmony and peace in your reality. I call this collapsing the field, a phrase that comes from my physics background. By your own volition to experience love and harmony, you can collapse the thoughts and emotions that you were using to empower your whirlybird.

For example, you may say or do something that you regret afterwards. The mind experiences guilt based on your self-judgment. Suddenly, you are off and running to create a Class Five tornado.

In my early years, when I struggled with guilt, within minutes of doing or conveying something good or bad, I would go into this painful pattern. Doing something good or not so good were equally effective at triggering this miserable pattern.

It was predictable and mean, contributing to my never feeling successful or enough. These whirlybirds always drained tremendous creative focus, causing my heart to feel frayed and inadequate. It prevented me from being successful because the consequence of success was exhausting.

I remember these whirlybirds driving me into exhaustion for days. I was certain I had done something wrong, but as I study the pattern, the truth is I could not have done anything right.

I no longer have this problem. I eventually learned to recognize when my mind was creating *too many words too fast*. I learned to say, "Stop! Too many words." Then I immediately asked myself what I was feeling and took my awareness to my emotional self.

I simply will not listen anymore to those racing thoughts. They hurt me, they hurt my body, and at best all they do is create chaos. Any decisions made while in this frantic state will perpetuate a chaotic reality.

I now make my decisions from a place of peace and harmony. If I am not in a place of balance, I simply tell myself or anyone asking for an answer that I need time to feel it. I love living this way. It took me many years to learn what I am sharing with you in this pearl of wisdom.

Do you create whirlybirds? . . ❧ . . What sets them off? . . ❧ . . Are you ready to learn how to collapse the field and eliminate them before they hurt you and your reality?

You can eliminate whirlybirds once your desire for harmony is greater than your desire to exhaust yourself with negative thoughts and emotions. You deserve to live this blessed peace.

Pearl Ninety-One

Fighting Authority

How many of you fight authority? . . . I feel most Americans are born with the tendency to fight rather than acknowledge another's authority. Authority is a tricky concept. If you cannot allow others to have authority in your world, your own personal authority is in jeopardy. It gives evidence that you are withholding your own inner authority that comes from God.

For example, if you have problems accepting that policemen have authority in terms of their protection of society, you will tend to create conflict with them, perhaps even wanting to take their authority away from them. This indicates that on a deeper level, you have beliefs and patterns that cause you to be insecure about your own authority. You will tend to fight with others who have authority rather than live the power of your own authority. You are diminished and less than your true potential because you waste your focus on taking authority from others rather than living the authority to be who you truly are as a being of love.

The authority figures with whom I battled most consistently were bureaucrats. The instant they told me I couldn't have what I wanted when I wanted it, I would succumb to the pattern. Before I had time to center myself, I had already blurted out a less-than loving comment to validate I was a victim and, in fact, a very angry one. I despised this pattern, and it took me years to finally overcome it.

As soon as I had unloaded my angry victim dialogue—which never assisted me in getting what I wanted when I wanted it anyway—I would say to myself, "I missed another opportunity to love." Interestingly, I displayed my temper and used words to express it only when this pattern surfaced. Normally, if I am hurt which is the cause of anger, I become quiet and say very little.

I love the way I handle bureaucrats now. Rather than feeling like a vulnerable, explosive rocket, I approach these situations with an open heart. I focus on receiving what I love and creating a warm interaction with the bureaucrat. This has been a normal way for me to interact with others for a long time, and I love bringing it in to this formerly uncomfortable situation.

Those of you who have strong authority issues will probably feel, "But if I let them have authority over me, they will control me. I will lose. I can't stand giving them authority." This is the illusion that authority issues create inside you. If you feel this, I can assure you with a hundred percent confidence that on some level you are insecure and seeking to diminish your own authority which comes from being connected to God as love and peace. Pain always results from this.

Until I could give bureaucrats authority to assist me, my efforts to wrest authority from them through my rage *always worked against me.* The instant that I became centered and trusted the bureaucrat's authority to support me, I was able to create a favorable situation.

Now, if the bureaucrat cannot provide what I am seeking to create, I warmly and respectfully acknowledge his or her authority and ask if they can provide alternatives. By acknowledging his or her authority, I grant full permission for its use to support my needs. From the powerful position of feeling respected and valued, he or she can then have the opportunity to creatively assist me.

They may recommend simply that I speak to their boss or take some other action. The important point is that they feel good about themselves, and so do I. I create the pleasure of loving their authority because it is assisting me. Additionally, I create a loving space for myself throughout the conversation, bringing pleasure to myself regardless of the outcome. This causes me to feel very powerful and able to express my full authority as a being of love.

For those of you who desire to heal your authority issues, I recommend that you first explore the payoffs for either keeping your authority issues or for healing them. Until you are clear that you truly want to heal this part of you, little is likely to occur. The next step to release the pattern is to heal the insecurity that does not want you to have powerful authority in your world. This authority comes from inside your heart and takes nothing away from another person's authority.

Do you fight the authority of the government or leaders of different organizations? . . 🌹. . What response patterns do you display when you are fighting authority? . . 🌹. . Are you willing to heal your authority issues? . . 🌹. . Do you desire to reclaim the powerful authority of an open, loving heart?

Until you make peace with authority figures, you are at war with your own authority as a being of love. Healing this within creates an environment of peace and supports a blessed and harmonious external world.

Pearl Ninety-Two

Once Is Too Often
to Hurl Meanness

When I teach, one of the first lessons is that it is never okay to be mean and hurl harsh words or feelings at others. Without exception, my students are cautioned that even though our families and society tell us it is okay to do this, it never is allowed when I teach. A single blow of harsh, angry, emotional words can damage a loving and open heart. Once this occurs, trust is lost, and the relationship lacks the ability to create the necessary safety and trust to support a blessed relationship.

Do you feel justified in verbally attacking another person? If so, your meanness will result in hurting and preventing the other person's heart from being open, trusting, and available to you.

That is a lot to sacrifice, because his or her trusting, open heart is how you experience love and sweetness in your external world. However, the price is even greater. Every time you hurl your pain at another person through harsh words, the wounds that probably exist in your heart and solar plexus which likely caused the attack tear even further. It makes it more difficult for you to receive the love you desire and perpetuates the illusion that it is the other person's fault.

I teach my students how to safely express powerful negative emotions without harm to themselves or others. If they feel they have issues with others, they learn to pull off the toxic, negative charge before they communicate. Otherwise, they might hurt the other person and damage the potential to create greater unity and trust in that relationship.

Lashing cathartic emotions at another person creates only hurt and separation. Often, if an individual examines true, deeper feelings rather than the surface rage caused by hurt, she or he finds the deepest desire is to give and receive love from the other person. Violent words or emotions can destroy the possibility of that love and trust.

For example, the following would create separation: "I am so angry at you that I can't stand you. Get out of my life." If an individual knew how to go deeply within their emotional self, he or she might better reflect his or her true feelings by saying, "I feel hurt because my heart desires to feel close to you and valued by you. When you don't include me, I feel disappointed and hurt that I am unable to create the closeness and love my heart desires with you. I miss you."

The first comments perpetuate the separation that hurt the individual in the first place. Little good will come of this. The second dialogue reflects a deeper level of truth about his or her true feelings. This tends to neutralize the pain and separation and to give clarity to the desire to connect and love. The second dialogue can move a person forward in a relationship, while the first dialogue can destroy it.

If you carry patterns of meanness, these patterns must be uplifted and removed if you desire to live a fuller expression of your heart. No matter how great your hurt, hurting another person only adds to it. Every time you hurl mean, blaming words, the person you are attacking trusts you less and creates a larger wall of separation as protection from you. The cost of this to you is tragic as it reduces your ability to receive love!

Some emotional-release schools of thought teach individuals to communicate their feelings by unloading rage and hatred on people they care about if that is what they feel. My teachings do not support this at all because it is so destructive. Often, when individuals work through the layer of rage and the underlying hurt, they find that the pain was generated by an inability to create love. Blasting individuals they desire to love with meanness and verbal abuse only deepens the separation that has created their pain.

Are you mean? . .✿. . Do you feel your meanness is necessary and justified? . .✿. . Have you faced how much damage you have done to yourself and others expressing meanness? . .✿. . Are you willing to give up the meanness and honestly create safety of the heart with those you love?

As beings of love, we must heal the part of us that creates patterns of meanness. Certainly, appropriate expressions of negative emotions can prevent us from hurting or harming self or others. The meanness that hurts others always hurts us as well.

Keeping What I Love

Pearl Ninety-Three

Destructiveness:
Avoid Creating It

Years ago, I drove a van that was safe, reliable, and maintenance-free. Although it was four years old and had many miles on it, the van looked new and had no mechanical problems. One evening, I read a book that suggested I was in a cycle that required destruction of what I had in order to build the new. At this time, I had already released my beautiful home and furnishings and was living off my savings. All that I really owned was my van. I questioned what I had to destroy.

The next day, I was driving my van, and in less than five minutes, I sensed something was wrong and looked down. The van had over-heated. Upset, I turned the engine off and pulled to the side of the road, sensing destruction everywhere. The fabric on the visor looked as though it had been stretched twenty times beyond its size. The rearview mirror was broken; several pieces that appeared to be in perfect condition now looked damaged and old.

As my overheated vehicle was towed, I remember having the thoughts that the only thing I owned at that time was my van. If I needed to destroy something to move myself forward, it would have to be my van. I had used information from a book to create its destruction in less than twenty-four hours.

I gained a lot of understanding from this. First, I learned that I create destruction in my life whether or not I am conscious of it, as in this case, or unaware of it. I recognized that destruction hurts and can be avoided. And I saw that the part of me that believed that it was loving to destroy my property was misprogrammed and definitely unsupportive of love. I also experienced how vulnerable I was to the suggestion of others.

Do you experience destruction in your life? . . ❦ . . Do you realize that you create that destructiveness? . . ❦ . . Is this destructiveness your highest choice or does it hurt you and create tremendous stress in your life? . . ❦ . . Are you willing to let go of the patterns that support destructiveness in your world?

Destroying something we love and value is always a choice within us. When we do, it creates stress and pain. Learning how to love ourselves more reduces this tendency.

Pearl Ninety-Four

Grabbing the Power and Running With It

As my overheated van approached the filling station, a sick feeling entered my stomach. When I talked to the mechanic, he said, "The engine's blown, and it will cost several thousand dollars to repair it." I left the van uncertain about what to do. As I walked home, fearful nauseating thoughts raced through my mind and body.

I thought, "I don't have several thousand dollars for a blown engine. I don't have a job. I don't have money. I don't have a car to go buy another car—I'm stranded with no hope. Alone, trapped, I may as well give up and die." By the time I got home, I could barely breathe. My labored breathing was not caused from the walk, but by fear.

I called the bank to inquire about interest rates. I had called a few months before to see if I could afford to replace my aging van. The interest had gone up two percent since I had called two months earlier when I first considered replacing the van. Panicking, I felt I had no options, and I harshly attacked myself for having waited until the interest rate had increased and my van was destroyed.

Suddenly, my inner guidance broke through my panic. "Grab the power exactly where you are, and run with it. Don't worry about what was or what isn't. You must grab the power now and run with it," the guidance repeated until I finally calmed down enough to listen.

I stood up and began pacing the room as I chanted, "Grab the power and run with it." Then, I would say, "But my down payment has a blown engine and the interest rates are up two percent." I would then stop myself, realizing that these thoughts gave away my power.

I would resynchronize myself as I moved with as much power as I could, again chanting, "Grab the power and run with it." After about twenty minutes, I could hold the power and sense what it felt like to know that I could handle what was before me, regardless of having little money, no job, and no other means of transportation.

As I sat down with a sense of my power, even in this difficult situation I had created, I felt I could create a workable solution. I called a friend who offered to help me shop for a new vehicle, and I accepted that the interest rate might be higher. I breathed deeply to relax from the painful stress I had created for myself.

As I sat there regrouping, the phone rang. It was the mechanic who called to tell me to come for my van. "Come get my van! What are you talking about? I have been in agony for the last hour about my van being destroyed, and you're telling me come get it—it's fine?" I said with shock in my voice. The mechanic, in good spirits, laughed as he said, "I don't know about your condition, lady, but your van is fine."

As I walked to the filling station, I explored what it meant to grab the power and run with it. I reviewed how I had felt when I had grabbed and held the power which I could only do when I was free of criticism and judgment. I realized that once the criticism and judgment began, I lost my power to fear and hopelessness. I felt how "what if" or "if I had" sucked the power away and left me weak.

Through this experience, I learned that it is important to grab my power exactly where I am at the moment I choose to create. As a result, I have been able to create manifestations that appear to be created out of nothing. By holding my power exactly where I am, regardless of the appearance that I am missing key ingredients to be able to create, everything seems to fall in place.

Do you take the power out of your creative manifestations with criticism and fear? . . ❦ . . Can you hold stable, knowing that you can handle any situation when difficult life experiences appear? . . ❦ . . Or do you choose to panic into patterns that validate that you have no hope or creative options?

If a situation appears to be hopeless, helpless, fearful, or without solutions remember:

Grab the power right where you are and run with it!

Pearl Ninety-Five

Giving Up What I Love

When I began my spiritual path, I fell prey to sacrificing what I love for God. Eventually, I gave up my beautiful home and furnishing, a social life that had always brought me joy, and wealth in order to pursue my spiritual desires. Although this choice was very painful, it did little to bring me closer to God. I believe I experienced this so that I could be absolutely clear about it with my students. I teach them, "You can pursue God in that way if you choose to. But it may hurt you if you do."

Before I gave up my home, I remember having the feeling that I could get closer to God if I could live in an empty room with no furniture. Two years later, I stayed at a primitive center for an entire summer, even though I had only planned to be there for two weeks. To make things worse, I had a condo on an island available to me. After about a month of sleeping on hard concrete floors on a futon, I saw clearly that I had created the empty room with a mat to sleep on based on a former desire to get close to God!

I was angry, fed up, and my back was in pain. I wanted a nice, soft bed with fluffy pillows and a down comforter. I learned from this experience that discomfort did not bring me closer to God because I was already close to God. I learned to neutralize beliefs that would hurt me if expressed.

There are many traditions that believe that releasing the physical, materialistic world will reconnect you with God. If that were true, our planet would be profoundly connected to God because so many beings live in poverty. This belief is simply a trick.

God is unlimited in terms of wealth, so, if this belief were true, once these impoverished people released their physical world, their God connection would become so powerful that they would want for nothing. It doesn't work that way, although I tricked myself into exploring this consciousness. When we believe that poverty is the way to God, poverty or denial of the physical world actually exhausts us and makes us want to die because of the struggle.

Also, this pattern keeps God stranded in our heads and blocked from entering into our hearts and physical creative world. It is one of those manifestations of physics. In truth, it is like allowing God to be present in part of us, but not in the part that has to do with our daily physical life. It was easy for me to get caught in these beliefs, and they hurt me and made me not want to live on Earth.

A much more powerful way of living is to love God and bring God's love into our physical world. That means God is available to help us express whatever style of living our heart chooses with wealth and abundance if we desire that. Giving up what we love in our physical world for God will hurt us and cause us to resent and fear God.

Our physical world today requires wealth to create rest, comfort, and well-being. Denial of that will hurt you. The truth I learned is that God's love is available to help us to create a blessed and abundant world to manifest our hearts' desires. When we do, we are full and free to generously express the God within us.

Had I read about this before I released my physical world, I probably would not have listened because I had such a huge desire to deeply learn all the nuances of this lesson. So, if you are convinced I am inaccurate, my heart sends you sweet blessings of comfort on your journey.

Does your mind stay in conflict about wealth and abundance as expressions of God's love or as something you should release in order to be close to God? . . ❧ . . Are you willing to bring peace to those conflicting parts of yourself? . . ❧ . . Do you have belief patterns that support disempowering yourself financially to control and limit yourself? . . ❧ . . Are you open to God's love assisting you in creating what you love on Earth?

Self-love gives us permission to infuse our world with the goodness and abundance that our hearts love. The more self-love that is present, the more effortless God's love flows through us.

Pearl Ninety-Six

Choosing Words

Have you ever observed the effect of different words on your feelings and body? Words are like mini-mental programs that tell the physical or emotional self how to respond. In other words, a specific word, which is really a sound vibration, will automatically tell our emotional and physical selves what program to play.

For example, slowly feel the words "warm water." Warm water is a wonderful set of words that tells our body and emotions to relax and allow ourselves to feel soothed and nurtured. Other words can do the opposite such as words that relate to terror, peril, or hopelessness. These words send in programs to our emotional or physical bodies that cause us to feel anxious.

With this awareness, we can choose words and word patterns that support us on an emotional and body level to feel empowered, safe, and supported versus words and word patterns that keep our body anxious and hypervigilant. Does your language to yourself and others support you feeling empowered, safe, and supported, or does it constantly keep you anxious and insecure? Responsibility for choosing words that feel good and support your well-being is within your reach and is a choice only you can make.

I would like to give an example of a word that I find consistently has a disempowering effect on me. To me, it constantly serves as a weight that holds down my power. If I say "just" I know immediately that I am suppressing my power to create what I love. "Just" is like a wet blanket I use to suppress a greater, more empowered reality. Whenever I choose to express my power as a being of love, I toss that word from my vocabulary!

When I say, "If I could 'just' be wealthy," I am actually limiting how much of God's love I allow into my body and world. I literally feel my solar plexus, where my power builds, knot up. I would be much more honest if I said, "I really want to stay financially disempowered." The "just" limits whatever it is attached to. It is definitely not a word that can support the abundance of my heart.

I "just" love her. Feel it. Notice that when you say "just" love her, you are reducing your power. Notice that it knots your tummy in a ball of restriction. If you want your full potential of love power, which is always linked with God's love, then say, "I love her." Notice how much freer this phrase is. It does not have the "just" to jam the power of your love.

Are you aware of the effect of words on the chemistry and energy of your body? . . ❦ . . Do you regularly use words that limit or cause you to feel insecure and disempowered? . . ❦ . . Or do you use language to express how greatly you love yourself and your power to express what you love?

It's a choice each of us has. The language of the heart takes us to a place of security and support through God's love that allows us to feel safe, available for life, and capable of living what we love.

Pearl Ninety-Seven

Punishment: I've Had Enough

Have you suffered enough? . . . Have you punished yourself enough to feel that you are complete with self-punishment? In order to know this, you must go very deeply within your heart. You will continue self-punishment until you reach that deep knowing within that you no longer desire to create or experience punishment from yourself or others.

So many individuals on Earth believe that they are bad without any concept of what they may have done. I remember as a child feeling so much guilt that I would confess to things I hadn't done. In truth, I wasn't the type that ever did anything obviously bad. However, I confessed to things in order to have some tangible reason for the unrelenting, inescapable feeling that I had done something wrong.

I must have felt there had to be a reason for the guilt, and since I didn't know what it was, I would manufacture one. Individuals with this kind of guilt typically display destructive actions that justify their guilt. It is a mean cycle that fosters more pain.

So often, the badness we feel guilty about is transferred to us through our ancestors. Until individuals learn about this kind of guilt and that it can be healed, they tend to be on automatic pilot for self-punishment. Because they feel they are "bad," they must perfect themselves by inflicting internal and external punishment. In truth, instead of creating perfection of the heart, mind, and body, it perpetuates pain and victimization that passes through the generations.

I remember the day that I knew that it didn't matter what I had done or what I hadn't done. Whatever it was, I had overpaid! From that moment, my focus shifted. I was committed to removing from my world anything that dealt with guilt, judgment, and punishment. When I would come to those places inside where guilt, judgment, and punishment would unleash themselves to harm me, I would say, "Stop. I've already punished myself way too much."

Every time I said that to myself, the momentum would cease. Shocked from the harshness of what I was doing to myself, I would stop, knowing that what I spoke was true. Each time I did this, it was like shaking an individual who was hitting his or her head against a wall to stop the destructive intent.

Once stopped, the individual wonders why he or she was doing it in the first place. When I would stop myself from the internal punishment, it felt as though I was waking from an ancient obsession about which I had no understanding or memory.

Does guilt and self-judgment create punishing patterns for you? . . 🌹 . . Have you over-punished yourself? . . 🌹 . . Do you desire to end your self-punishment?

> It doesn't matter what you have done.
> It doesn't matter what you haven't done.
> You are a being of love and deserve love!

Only you can decide when you are ready to live this truth and when you desire to free yourself from the pain of punishment, judgment, and guilt. When you are ready, say to the guilt, "Stop, whatever punishment I have desired, I have overpaid."

Pearl Ninety-Eight

When I Can't Afford
to Be Scared

What if you are in a situation that is threatening and potentially harmful? Write out exactly what you want to happen as the most optimistic, high integrity, and self-loving outcome. I have successfully used this creative ability for two tax audits. In each one, I obtained exactly what I asked for. This is a powerful way to recover your power in a situation that has the potential to hurt you, or a situation in which you may feel victimized.

In the first instance where my taxes were audited, I had been very honest in completing the forms, but some deductions were risky because the IRS had been nebulous and problematic about this particular area. Based on IRS statistics, these deductions might or might not be allowed.

As I felt the situation, I knew that I could not afford the deductions to be disclaimed. I decided to create my tax audit as an opportunity to love. I knew that by holding my desire for my audit to be an opportunity to love, I would create my highest probability that the deductions would be allowed. In other words, having the IRS agree with my deductions would protect my finances, and this would support experiencing love in my world.

Every time I thought of my audit, I would remind myself that it was an opportunity to love. When I arrived at the IRS office the day of my audit with a box of receipts and validations of my deductions, a soft-spoken, sweet lady quietly guided me into her office. She said she wanted me to relax and explained how difficult it was on her that people were afraid of her and her job.

Soon, our hearts were wide open as we established a loving and mutually sweet rapport. We discussed how we liked to love and help people feel safe and comfortable, and I left the office with a full heart enriched by my opportunity to love. My financial reward was that I was required to pay less than a hundred dollars in a potentially expensive situation.

As the sweet lady was verifying my deductions, I overheard the exchange between a couple and an IRS agent behind us. The three of them were screaming at each other at the top of their lungs. They appeared to barely avoid a physical fight. Each had mutually chosen to create an opportunity for fighting, rage, and hate.

The audited couple were challenged on every detail. I could hear the demands from the agent requiring them to provide verification down to the penny. Their audit was financially painful; filled with war, hatred, and perceived victimization; and allowed no benefit of doubt. The IRS agent and the couple hated each other, and each wanted to hurt the other. Everyone got what he or she desired to create, which was an opportunity to fight and hate. Wow, what a costly choice!

My other audit was related to an extremely difficult personal growth process that required developing patterns for myself to transfer the seat of my power from my mind to my heart. Through this, I was learning how to assist my students in doing the same.

I asked God that once I completed my personal self-growth work, I wanted the IRS person to have no interest in reviewing my records. I focused on the personal transformational work which had brought this audit into my life. This process required healing that part of myself that inappropriately valued my mind far more than it valued my heart.

Once this deep inner healing occurred, I did my homework to prepare for the audit. I learned in this audit to organize my records so that any auditing in the future would require no additional preparation time on my part. I walked into the IRS office with my accountant. The agent took us into her office and explained that although I was randomly chosen, her review of my taxes indicated it would be a waste of the government's time to do anything further. My accountant and I shook hands with her, and I walked out of the office knowing that, once again, I had created exactly what I had asked for.

When I initially received the audit notice, I knew it was an alert that a deep personal issue was ready to be healed. The painful feelings associated with this audit showed me where to focus healing transformations deep within. My uncomfortable feelings about the audit gave me the map of where my power was not valuing my heart. This was a huge victory for me as a soul.

Often, experiences that appear to be one thing, such as a tax audit, are related on a deeper level to complex aspects of ourselves seeking to be healed or dealt with in new and more loving ways. In truth, we are not victims of our creations, although we can easily feel or believe that. Once the healing transformation takes place, the experience has no further impact. Or, as in my case, it sets in motion blessings that were not available until this deep inner healing was completed.

Do you create life events to express exactly what you desire to experience, or do you hopelessly become a victim of what looks like unlucky fate? . . . Do you use your power to love yourself to help you through potentially disruptive situations? . . . Or do you go into fear, blaming, and fighting with the very person that has the ability to hurt you? . . . Are you ready to shift this?

Creating something you love is always a choice. It is up to you whether life events are pain-filled or express what you desire. Creating "an opportunity to love" in challenging life events is a great way to use love to support what you desire to live.

Pearl Ninety-Nine

Choosing Life

Unless individuals live what their hearts' love, they create and experience pain. If they create enough suffering, they will want to escape the hurt. As they desire to escape anguish, they will create escapes, such as addictions and drowning their awareness through over-working or watching television excessively. As their misery builds, so does their desire to die.

Our minds are smart. When they see us suffering, they have a simple solution. Die. Death will get you out of this mess. Out of mercy, our minds will set in motion a way to end the misery. Dying is a perfectly logical solution to pain in our physical lives. The manner of death doesn't matter much—perhaps an accident, a quick disease, or a slow, subtle type of disease that wears you down.

Once our minds try to help us end the pain by dying, our creative energy, which could be used to create bliss and amazing lives, focuses on ending life. You are set on a course of misery, and you have less and less life-force. Your life obviously works less and less well as the program to die gains more and more of your focus. Some people are not even aware that they are doing this. Others know they are, but feel helpless to do anything about it.

You can turn this around. Sometimes individuals already have one foot in death's doorway. However, once they feel the beauty and power of actually being able to live what their hearts love, they abandon their desire to die and substitute a new desire to live life fully. These individuals outlive their doctors' dire predictions, and every day gets warmer and more fulfilling for them. As a teacher, I love to help people turn from that much suffering to open their hearts and lives.

I have no judgment if someone truly wants to die. I bless and release them. However, no one should die because the available information limited his or her choices. If a person does not understand the power of self-love, then they can easily be vulnerable to desiring to die. Our world can simply be too painful and harsh without self-love. That's part of the reason I teach self-love. I daily watch its amazing ability to uplift not only my life but also the lives of those around me.

Are you choosing to live fully with all your creative energy focused toward creating what you love? . . . Or are you in so much pain that you perceive death as a merciful relief? . . . If so, are you willing to explore the possibility of learning to love yourself? . . . Or have you simply given up?

Our minds can be a great blessing to us if properly programmed to support that. Healing the desire to die because of pain opens the doorway for your mind to support you living what you love. This delightful option is rich and fulfilling.

Pearl One Hundred

Dissolving Nervous Habits

O ne day I had lunch with one of my students. Her nervous tearing of napkins, fidgeting with her food, and compulsively organizing the M&M's into color-coordinated piles shifted the conversation to her nervous habits.

She shared with me that these were a few of her many nervous habits. She had been unsuccessful in changing these bothersome behaviors, and she asked if I had any suggestions. Since I hadn't thought much about such behavior, I didn't have any suggestions. We laughed a little about her habits, and then continued onto a new topic of conservation.

However, as I sat next to her, I began feeling the different patterns that were causing each of these nervous habits. Once I could identify the causes, I was able to provide affirmations that would shift her perception and loyalty away from the abusive patterns. We quickly scratched the affirmations on what was left of her tattered napkin. I suggested that she say them each time she was aware that she was doing the nervous habit, and, in addition, at the beginning of each day.

It was amazing! Within a week, these nervous patterns which she had experienced most of her life were erased. The next time we were together, she asked for affirmations to eliminate other nervous habits. Within a week or so, she was free of these patterns, too. After that, other students began asking for affirmations to help them release their nervous behaviors.

Since I am unable to individually feel what is causing your nervous habits, I believe that it might be helpful to give you a few general affirmations based on my experience with helping others. If you have a nervous habit you would like to eliminate, sense with your intuition which affirmation is best for you. Say it several times a day as well as when you are aware of doing the nervous habit. Within ten days of this, you should see results. If you don't, consider choosing a different affirmation. Good luck!

Here are some affirmations to eliminate nervous habits:

> I love myself, and trust myself to create love.
> I love the Earth, and I love being alive, healthy, and creative on the Earth.
> I trust myself, I trust God, and I trust love.
> I am a being of love. I trust unity with myself, God, and humanity.
> When I am afraid, I relax, and trust myself and God.
> I love my creativity, and use it to create joy for myself.
> I am safe and protected because I love myself and I am loved by God.

Works of Tanai Starrs

	U.S.	Canada
Books:		
Pearls of Heart Wisdom	$21.95	$29.50
Creating the Sacred Child	23.95	32.00
God's Physics That Will Touch Your Heart	21.95	29.50
Power to Heal	21.95	29.50
CD's and Cassettes:		
Transformational Bedtime Stories for Adults, *(2-cass)*	21.95	29.50
Transformational Bedtime Stories for Adults, *(2-CDs)*	23.95	32.00
Wonders of My Inner Child *(music)*	15.00	20.00
Initiation to Love *(music)*	15.00	20.00
Soothing My Pain *(words and music)*	15.00	20.00

Events, Seminars, and Schools

Please visit website at
www.tanaistarrs.com

PO Box 8039
Asheville, NC 28814

Order Form

Please fill out the following form, completely and legibly. Mail to Joy Heart or call (800) 996-3018. Wholesale discounts available. You may also order at www.tanaistarrs.com.

Name_____

Address_____

City_____ State_____

Country_____ Postal Code_____

Phone_____ FAX_____

E-mail_____

Credit card_____Exp Date_____

Or check or money order_____

Thank you,

Tanai Starrs

ABOUT THE AUTHOR
Tanai Starrs

Tanai Starrs is an international heart teacher who helps individuals open their hearts to live what they love. Tanai is founder of the Joy Heart Corporation, an educational company to support living a heart-centered life. She also co-founded The Mastery of the Heart School, a three-year program, which began in 1994.

Tanai has assisted individuals to walk beyond fear into profound empowerment, living the beauty, sacredness, and creativity of an open heart. She has appeared on television including the Wisdom Channel with her teachings. The success of her teaching has assisted individuals in walking beyond dying, limitation, and despair into health, joy, and abundance.

With an M.S. in biochemistry, Tanai worked as an engineer and scientist for 20 years at two major U.S. corporations before co-founding her school. Tanai did 18 years of private study and research on how to use science to create an open heart and purified genetics capable of creating high self-esteem, success, and empowerment.

Tanai is also a musician and storyteller. She uses her creativity to assist in teaching and helping her students to integrate complex understandings in a simple and engaging way. One of her loves is to transform science so her students have a heart experience that supports joy and deep understanding. In this way, she moves science beyond a mental concept into a body and feeling experience that creates magical wonder that intrigues and delights her audiences.

A Look Into Other Works
by Tanai Starrs

Transformational Bedtime Stories for
Adults, and Children Too: Volume I

What are adults to do who have lost the magic they felt as children? Are their hearts fated to remain locked? Where are the stories for adults that awaken their dreams? Where are the stories that touch the inner child buried deep within? Author Tanai Starrs asked these questions one day and to her delight, *Transformational Bedtime Stories for Adults, Vol. I* was birthed. Using her abilities as a storyteller, musician, and spiritual teacher, Tanai created these magical poems and stories to reawaken the sensual, feeling realm of the inner child.

Relax and allow the magic of these archetypal stories to awaken awareness hidden deep within. Delight as a child would in the simple, singsong poetry that was written to touch the heart, not the intellect. Allow the questions of the poems to activate your subconscious and help you to create a more fulfilling life.

Children are passionate when they feel love, anger, sadness, joy, excitement, frustration, jealousy, pride, and sometimes rage and distaste. Until they learn to judge their feelings and to control and limit them, their emotions are powerfully expressed. Give yourself permission to be truly emotionally honest. Then give yourself the freedom to go deeply into the story and poetry, allowing and expressing your emotions as a child would. Feel it all fully. As you do, you begin to regain your inner child.

Let your story time contain the emotional richness and openness of a trusting child in this magical opportunity to awaken the heart in both adults and children.

Enjoy Tanai's music from instrumental CDs, *Wonders of My Inner Child and Victories of My Heart* as background for these delightful stories.

Power to Heal

September 11, 2001 changed our nation. Rather than terrorists, we Americans must define these changes. *Power to Heal* helps us face these changes and define them so that we heal and restore what we lost—becoming greater than before as a people and nation.

Power to Heal causes us to empower ourselves through our country's great founding principle: "In God We Trust." As we renew this birthright, *Power to Heal* assists in healing our wounds in order to walk beyond our fears so we may create what we desire rather than allow the harmful intent of terrorism.

The destructive force of terror sent us, our financial structure, and our country into a state of shock, uncertainty, confusion, loss, and fear that diminished how we do business. In order for us to move forward without this damage holding us back, we must individually and as a nation free our financial structure from shock, uncertainty, confusion, loss, and fear. As long as those patterns are influencing how we generate wealth, terrorism has continuing power to influence our financial stability and well-being. *Power to Heal* gives a roadmap through our healing to reclaim our financial security and power.

Terrorism is the ultimate violation of the power of peace through debilitating fear and dread. Resolution of terrorism is not complete until our hearts are restored to trust that our peace has power. *Power to Heal* is a unique restructuring roadmap out of fear and wounding to empowered peace that supports our enhanced success.

This book helps us to reduce stress and assists us in coping with a fast-paced world which now has terrorism adding to its complexity.

Creating the Sacred Child

Is the quality of a child's genetics, and therefore his or her life, an act of fate or may we as loving parents enhance the genetic quality of our children? In *Creating the Sacred Child*, Tanai discusses how to create extraordinary children with expanded abilities in love, creativity, leadership, and empowerment.

With the recent interest in the Genome genetic project, this timely book provides profound healing opportunities and new awareness of how connection to God as love can be passed from one generation to the next. Without a heart connection coded in the genetics, the next generation is fated to replay the fear, pain, and lack their parents experienced. The possibility of positively influencing your child's genetics is a gift of knowledge not to be missed.

In *Creating the Sacred Child*, Tanai reveals clear self-help instructions in allowing sacredness into conception, pregnancy, birth, and the raising or releasing of a child. In an understandable way, this book teaches how we may positively influence the genetics of our children whether we give birth to them or adopt them.

Tanai provides a beautiful perspective on adoption, which heals the hearts of parents unable to birth children, parents releasing their children for adoption, and adopted children. *Creating the Sacred Child* is the book parents have been waiting for who desire to create and raise extraordinary children of love, both adopted and natural.

"My wife and son are alive today because of her teachings!"
—*Robert Murri: Asheville, NC*

"I feel so blessed to be my daughter's mother. Our souls have merged to a level of relationship I never believed possible thanks to Tanai's teachings."
—*Sharlie Watts: Ridgway, CO*

"My work with Tanai has freed me from attachments, allowing me to release my children to their dreams, as I begin to discover my own."
—*Kris Johnson-Ayers: Oakland, CA*

God's Physics That Will Touch Your Heart

Must science remain in the hands of the mental elite? *God's Physics That Will Touch Your Heart* provides an original model of science of the heart, which may be used by anyone desiring to uplift their daily lives. This book has been described as the "feminine approach to science." The beauty of this heart science is that it teaches individuals to master their physical, emotional, mental, and spiritual selves to create what they love.

God's Physics That Will Touch Your Heart opens the doorway to the forefront of new consciousness by guiding the reader to experience and feel complex scientific concepts such as gravity, refraction, particle-wave and the multi-dimensional nature of energy, and the superstring theory (currently, the most successful modern physics theory) through heart-opening stories, simple pictures, and personal scientific experiences. Rather than a cold mental concept of science, *God's Physics That Will Touch Your Heart* allows readers to feel and experience science as warm, alive, understandable, uplifting, and available to bless every moment of their lives.

God's Physics That Will Touch Your Heart presents science in a way that can teach people how to walk out of guilt and self-abuse so they may connect to God as unlimited love. The book provides a warmth and connection to the heart that people long to experience. The scientific as well as nonscientific student will equally delight in this powerful, warm, engaging, and transformational approach.